SKILL
SHARPENERS

Third Edition

2

JUDY DeFILIPPO
CHARLES SKIDMORE

Longman

Judy DeFilippo supervises MATESL student teachers at Simmons College in Boston, Massachusetts. She is the author of *Lifeskills 1, 2,* and *3* and co-author of *Grammar Plus.*

Charles Skidmore is the principal of Arlington High School in Arlington, Massachusetts. He has taught and supervised the teaching of English as a Second Language for the past twenty-five years. He also serves as adjunct faculty in the Lynch School of Education at Boston College.

Pearson Education, 10 Bank Street, White Plains, NY 10606

Vice president, primary and secondary editorial: Ed Lamprich
Senior development editor: Virginia Bernard
Vice president, design and production: Rhea Banker
Director of editorial production: Linda Moser
Production supervisor: Melissa Leyva
Associate production editor: Laura Lazzaretti
Marketing managers: Alex Smith, Tania Saiz-Sousa
Senior manufacturing buyer: Dave Dickey
Cover design: Ann France
Cover photo: © Emma Lee/Life File/Getty Images
Text design adaptation: Tracey Munz Cataldo
Text composition: Laserwords
Text font: 11/18 Myriad Roman
Illustrations: Elizabeth Hazelton, Kathleen Todd, Andrew Lange
Photo credits: National Aeronautics and Space Administration, p. 68;
    Library of Congress, pp. 76 and 105

ISBN: 0-13-192993-3
Printed in the United States of America
1 2 3 4 5 6 7 8 9 10–VHG–08 07 06 05 04

Introduction

The *Skill Sharpeners* series has been especially designed for students whose skills in standard English, especially those skills concerned with literacy, require strengthening. It is directed both toward students whose first language is not English and toward those who need additional practice in standard English grammar and vocabulary. By introducing basic skills tied to classroom subjects in a simple, easy-to-understand grammatical framework, the series helps to prepare these students for success in regular ("mainstream") academic subjects. By developing and reinforcing school and life survival skills, it helps build student confidence and self esteem.

Skills Sharpeners focuses on grammar practice and higher order thinking skills. It provides many content-area readings, biographies, opportunities for students to write, and practice in using formats similar to those of many standardized tests. The third edition updates the content of many pages. The central purpose of the series remains the same, however. *Skill Sharpeners* remains dedicated to helping your students sharpen their skills in all facets of English communication.

With English Language Learners, *Skill Sharpeners* supplements and complements any basic ESL text or series. With these students and with others, *Skill Sharpeners* can also be used to reteach and reinforce specific skills with which students are having—or have had—difficulty. In addition, it can be used to review and practice grammatical structures and to reinforce, expand, and enrich students' vocabularies.

The grammatical structures and the language objectives in *Skill Sharpeners* follow a systematic, small-step progression with many opportunities for practice, review, and reinforcement. Vocabulary and skill instruction is presented in the context of situations and concepts that have an immediate impact on students' daily lives. Themes and subject matter are directly related to curriculum areas. Reading and study skills are stressed in many pages, and writing skills are carefully developed, starting with single words and sentences and building gradually to paragraphs and stories in a structured, controlled composition sequence.

Skill Sharpeners is an ideal supplement for literature-based or sheltered English classrooms. *Skill Sharpeners* allows for direct teaching of grammar and language skills that most textbooks and novels do not supply. Students do not always intuitively grasp grammar and language rules. *Skill Sharpeners* has been designed to allow students a vehicle for continued practice in these areas.

Using the *Skill Sharpeners*

Because each page or pair of pages of the *Skill Sharpeners* is independent and self contained, the series lends itself to great flexibility of use. Teachers may pick and choose pages that fit the needs of particular students, or they may use the pages in sequential order. Most pages are self-explanatory, and all are easy to use, either in class or as homework assignments. Annotations at the bottom of each page identify the skill or skills being developed and suggest ways to prepare for, introduce, and present the exercise(s) on the page. In most cases, oral practice of the material is suggested before the student is asked to complete the page in writing. Teacher demonstration and student involvement and participation help build a foundation for completing the page successfully and learning the skill.

Skill Sharpeners is divided into thematic units. The first unit of each book is introductory. In *Skill Sharpeners 1*, this unit provides exercises to help students say and write their names and addresses and to familiarize them with basic classroom language, school deportment, the names of school areas and school personnel, and number names. In later books of the series, the first unit serves both to review some of the material taught in earlier books and to provide orientation to the series for students coming to it for the first time.

At the end of each of the *Skill Sharpeners* books is a review of vocabulary and an end-of-book test of grammatical and reading skills. The test, largely in multiple-choice format, not only assesses learning of the skills but also provides additional practice for other multiple-choice tests.

The Table of Contents in each book identifies the skills developed on each page. An Index at the end of the book provides an alphabetical list of language objectives. The language objectives are also displayed prominently at the top of each page.

Skill Sharpeners invites expansion! We encourage you to use them as a springboard and to add activities and exercises that build on those in the books to fill the needs of your own particular students. Used this way, the *Skill Sharpeners* can significantly help to build the confidence and skills that students need to be successful members of the community and successful achievers in subject-area classrooms.

Contents

UNIT 1   Likes and Dislikes

Completing Forms (*Reading a driver's license, completing identification forms, reading dates*) 1

Questions and Answers (*Reviewing basic grammar, vocabulary, and sentence structure*) 2

Match the Columns (*Building vocabulary, classifying*) 3

Meet the Garza Family (*Reviewing present form of* to be, *present progressive, forming questions*) 4

What's for Lunch? (*Present tense, third-person singular:* likes/doesn't like) 5

What Do You Like? (*Reviewing simple present tense, asking/ answering questions with* do/does ... like/like to) 6

Fannee Doolee's Secret (*Classifying, deductive thinking*) 7

A Chat (*Reading for details, sequencing*) 8

Reading a Graph (*Interpreting a bar graph*) 9

What's Wrong? (*Reviewing the present progressive, writing a paragraph from a picture*) 10

Helping You Study: the Table of Contents (*Using a Table of Contents, interpreting chapter titles*) 11

Dear Dot (*Reading comprehension, understanding words through context, making judgments*) 12

UNIT 2   Careers and Activities

What Do They Do? (*Reviewing the simple present tense, building vocabulary*) 13

What Do You Want to Be? (*Present tense:* want(s) to) 14

Choosing a Career (*Using* like(s) to, want(s) to, has/have to, *reading for details, writing a paragraph*) 15

What's Their Job? (*Identifying topics, building vocabulary, drawing conclusions, writing a paragraph*) 16

What, Where, and *Why?* (*Reviewing the present progressive tense*) 17

Present or Present Progressive? (*Contrasting the present tenses*) 18

Helping You Study: Alphabetical Order (1) (*Alphabetizing by first and second letters*) 19

Helping You Study: Alphabetical Order (2) (*Alphabetizing*) 20

Dear Dot (*Reading comprehension, understanding words through context, making judgments*) 21

UNIT 3   Always, Sometimes, Never

A Day in the Life of Ernest (*Interpreting a chart, understanding adverbs of frequency, third-person singular present tense*) 22

Odd Man Out (*Classifying, using adverbs of frequency*) 23

Life in a Fire Station (*Identifying main idea and details, understanding adverbs of frequency*) 24

Depositing a Check (*Reading a check, understanding bank procedures*) 25

Opening a Savings Account (*Learning about savings accounts, understanding entries in a statement*) 26

A Student Survey (*Interpreting a chart, using adverbs of frequency*) 27

Is That a Fact? (*Distinguishing between fact and opinion*) 28

Have or *Has*? (*Present forms of* to have, *reading for details*) . . . . **.29**

Helping You Study: Using the Dictionary (1)
    (*Approximating the location of a word in the dictionary*) . . . . **.30**

Dear Dot (*Reading comprehension, understanding words*
    through context, making judgments) . . . . **.31**

UNIT 4   Busy Lives

Dr. Schwartz's Schedule (*Third-person singular,*
    simple present tense, asking questions) . . . . **.32**

Things People Do (*Constructing third-person*
    singular present tense: -s, -es) . . . . **.33**

How They Live: Two Stories (*Constructing the*
    present tense, choosing the correct form) . . . . **.34**

Writing About a Job (*Third-person singular present*
    tense: -s, -es, -ies, identifying main idea) . . . . **.35**

Whose Is It? (*Using possessive nouns and adjectives*) . . . . **.36**

The 911 Operator (*Learning about 911,*
    reading for details) . . . . **.37**

Do, Does, Don't, Doesn't (*Simple present tense with* do/does) . . . . **.38**

Families (*Identifying topics, understanding characters' feelings*) . . . . **.39**

A Future Job (*Learning about job openings and salaries in*
    the United States, adding to find a total, subtracting
    to find the difference) . . . . **.40**

What Are They Doing? (*Drawing conclusions, reviewing*
    the present progressive tense, building vocabulary) . . . . **.41**

Helping You Study: Using the Dictionary (2)
    (*Using guide words*) . . . . **.42**

Dear Dot (*Reading comprehension, understanding words*
    through context, making judgments, writing a letter) . . . . **.43**

UNIT 5   Making Plans and Solving Problems

Vacation Plans (*Future form:* be going to, *reading travel*
    ads, asking/answering questions, writing a paragraph) **44–45**

The Festival of Las Fallas (*Identifying main idea and details*) . . . . **.46**

Choose the Right Word (*Using prepositions*) . . . . **.47**

What Are They Going to Do? (*Making predictions,*
    creative problem solving) **48–49**

In, On, Under (*Using prepositional phrases, classifying*) . . . . **.50**

A Good Friend (*Identifying main idea and details,*
    making inferences, sequencing) . . . . **.51**

Helping You Study: Alphabetical Order (3)
    (*Listing people alphabetically by last names*) . . . . **.52**

Dear Dot (*Reading comprehension, understanding*
    words through context, making judgments, writing a letter) **53**

UNIT 6   Yesterday and Long Ago

Only Joking (*Understanding riddles*) . . . . **.54**

The Simple Past Tense (*Forming past tense of*
    regular verbs, writing sentences) . . . . **.55**

What Did They Do? (*Forming simple past tense,*
    pronunciation of final -ed) . . . . **.56**

How Does It Sound? (*Simple past tense,*
    distinguishing among the three sounds of -ed) . . . . **.57**

Adding -ed (*Forming simple past tense, observing spelling changes*) . . . . **.58**

A Time Line (*Interpreting and charting a time line*) . . . . **.59**

It's a Record! (*Reading comprehension: building vocabulary, using simple past tense*) 60–61
Helping You Study: Using the Encyclopedia (*Selecting the correct encyclopedia volume, alphabetizing*) 62
When Did It Happen? (*Interpreting a time line, sequencing*) 63
Dear Dot (*Reading comprehension, understanding words through context, making judgments, writing a letter*) 64

UNIT 7   Yesterday and Today
Irregular Past Tense (*Using irregular past tense verbs, writing sentences*) 65
What's the Problem? (*Solving mathematical word problems*) 66
The Present and Past of *to be* (*Present tense of* to be, *comparing uses of the present and past tense*) 67
Sally Ride (*Reading a chart, asking questions*) 68
An Unlucky Day (*Using the simple past and past progressive tenses*) 69
Tina's Terrible Trip (*Using the simple past and past progressive tenses*) 70
Susan B. Anthony: Fighting for People's Rights (*Reading a biography, making inferences, learning test-taking skills*) 71
Feelings (*Interpreting characters' feelings, building vocabulary*) 72–73
Dear Dot (*Reading comprehension, understanding words through context, making judgments, writing a letter*) 74

UNIT 8   People and Places
Armando's Week (*Interpreting a school schedule*) 75
Helen Keller (*Reading a biography, building vocabulary, understanding regular and irregular past tense*) 76–77
Combining Sentences (*Combining sentences with* and, but, *and* so) 78
In the Library (*Building vocabulary, learning about library resources*) 79
Don Roberts, Delivery Man (*Reviewing past tense, telling a story from picture cues, writing a paragraph*) 80
Choose the Verb Form (*Comparing uses of verb tenses: simple present and past, present and past progressive, and future* (going to)) 81
Helping You Study: Alphabetical Order (4) (*Alphabetizing book titles*) .82
Jesse James, a Famous Outlaw (*Reading a biography, building vocabulary, distinguishing between fact and opinion*) 83
Dear Dot (*Reading comprehension, understanding words through context, making judgments, writing a letter*) 84

UNIT 9   Agree and Disagree
Commands (*Recognizing imperatives, drawing conclusions*) 85
Opposites (*Recognizing opposites, learning test-taking skills*) 86
How Does It Work? (*Reading a technical article, interpreting a diagram, making inferences, sequencing*) 87
I Disagree! (*Recognizing opposites, building vocabulary*) 88

Helping You Study: Using the Card Catalog
(*Locating card catalog entries*) **89**
Emergency! (*Following directions, using imperatives,
understanding words through context*) **90**
Which One Is Correct? (*Reviewing simple present
tense, using adjective clauses with* who *and* that) **91**
Dear Dot (*Reading comprehension, understanding words
through context, making judgments, writing a letter*) **92**

UNIT 10   Reading Maps, Following Directions

The Fifty States (*Reading for detail, distinguishing between
fact and opinion, completing true/false/? statements*) **93**
A Map of the United States (*Interpreting a political map,
categorizing, learning/writing about a state*) **94–95**
The United States: a Geography Lesson (*Identifying
main idea and details, interpreting a topographic map*) . . . **96**
Travels with Charley (*Reading for details, making
inferences, learning test-taking skills*) **97**
Street Directions (*Reading a city map, following and
writing street directions*) **98–99**
Helping You Study: What Kind of Book? (*Understanding
library classification*) **100**
What Were They Doing? (*Using the past progressive tense,
drawing conclusions*) **101**
Dear Dot (*Reading comprehension, understanding words
through context, making judgments, writing a letter*) **102**

UNIT 11   Our Country and Climate

What's the Weather? (*Reading a weather map, using
Fahrenheit temperatures, reviewing weather vocabulary*) . . . **103**
What's the Temperature? (*Reading and computing
Fahrenheit temperatures*) **104**
Thomas Paine (*Reading a biography, reading for detail,
making inferences, learning test-taking skills*) **105**
The United States Government (*Reading comprehension,
building vocabulary, identifying main idea and details,
choosing the appropriate definition*) **106–107**
Helping You Study: Using an Index (*Using a book index*) . . . **108**
Places and People (*Using* who *clauses, building vocabulary*) . . **109**
Find the Ending (*Reading comprehension, understanding
adjective clauses with* who, where, what) **110**
Dear Dot (*Reading comprehension, understanding words
through context, making judgments, writing a letter*) **111**

Vocabulary Review **112–115**

End of Book Tests

Completing Familiar Structures **116–117**
Writing Questions **118**
Reading Comprehension **119**

Index of Language Objectives **120**

A **Answer the questions. Use short answers. The first one is done for you.**

NEW YORK STATE DRIVER LICENSE

Richard E. Spaulding
Commissioner of Motor Vehicles
ID: 777 965 211

DOB: **06-12-86**
TORRES, RAFAELA, X.
333 VALLEY RD
NEW TOWN NY 19087
SEX: **F** EYES: **BR** HT: **5-05** CLASS: **D**
E:
ISSUED: **07-25-04** EXPIRES: **02-07-07**
8645321

1. What is her first name?   Rafaela
2. What is her last name?   _____
3. What is her address?   _____
4. What is her license number? _____
5. What is her date of birth? _____
6. What is the expiration date? _____

B **Now complete the sentences about you, and fill in the form.**

STUDENT I.D. CARD

Please Print

Mr.   Miss
Mrs. Ms.   Name _____
                 (last)   (first)   (middle)
Address: _____
                    (street)
_____
   (city)   (state)   (zip)
Home Telephone: _____ Sex: M F
Native Country: _____
Signature: _____

1. My first name is _____
2. My address is _____
3. My date of birth is _____
4. My native country is _____

C **Write the dates.**

1. 3 – 4 – 90   March 4, 1990
   month day year
2. 10–10–66   _____
3. 8–30–79   _____
4. 1–21–04   _____

Questions and Answers

**Answer the following questions in your notebook.
Use complete sentences.**

Set A

1. What is your first name?
2. What is your last name?
3. Do you have a nickname? What is it?
4. Where do you live?
5. How old are you?
6. What time do you wake up in the morning?
7. What time do you go to bed at night?
8. What time do you eat lunch on Monday?
9. What time do you eat lunch on Saturday?
10. What time do you eat dinner?
11. Where are you from?
12. What are you wearing today?
13. How many people are there in your family?
14. How many brothers do you have?
15. How many sisters do you have?
16. What is your favorite color?
17. What do you like to do after school?
18. What do you look like?
19. What is your telephone number?
20. What are some of your favorite foods?
21. What sports or games do you like to play?
22. What is your native language?

Set B

1. What letter comes before *L* in the alphabet?
2. What number comes after 7?
3. How many pennies are there in a dime?
4. How many dimes are there in a dollar?
5. How many nickels are there in a quarter?
6. What's the weather like today?
7. When do you use an umbrella?
8. What are the four seasons of the year?
9. What month comes after June?
10. What month comes before February?
11. How many states are there in the United States?
12. What are the four directions on a map?
13. What part of the country do you live in?
14. What day comes after Tuesday?
15. What day comes before Saturday?
16. Who takes care of sick people in a hospital?
17. What does a mechanic do?
18. How much does it cost to make a call at a pay phone?

SKILL OBJECTIVE: Reviewing basic grammar, vocabulary, and sentence structure. Students' answers to these questions will provide information about their language abilities at the present time. You may wish to do the page orally first, either as a class exercise or as pair work, and then assign it for independent written work in class or at home.

Match the Columns

Read carefully. Find the best word in Column B to go with Column A. Write it next to the word in Column A. The first one is done for you.

A   **B**

Country   **Language**

1. Australia   _English_   Greek

2. Mexico   _____   Arabic

3. China   _____   ~~English~~

4. Greece   _____   Portuguese

5. Brazil   _____   Dutch

6. Saudi Arabia   _____   Chinese

7. Netherlands   _____   Spanish

Occupation   **Place**

1. teacher   _____   restaurant

2. nurse   _____   classroom

3. mail clerk   _____   business office

4. office assistant   _____   orchestra

5. mechanic   _____   hospital

6. chef   _____   post office

7. musician   _____   gas station

Food Item   **Food Category**

1. banana   _____   meat

2. lemonade   _____   dessert

3. carrot   _____   seafood

4. ice cream   _____   poultry

5. beef   _____   drink

6. clams   _____   vegetable

7. chicken   _____   fruit

SKILL OBJECTIVES: Building vocabulary; classifying. Preview the vocabulary and teach or review any unfamiliar or difficult words. You may wish to do several items orally as a class before assigning the page for independent written work. Encourage students to use a dictionary if they encounter an unknown word. Discuss the completed page with the class. For additional practice, have students put the word pairs into question/answer form, for example, "In what country or countries do people speak English?" and ask and answer the questions with a partner.

Meet the Garza Family

Read the story.

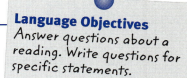

Language Objectives
Answer questions about a reading. Write questions for specific statements.

Everyone in the Garza family has a talent. Mr. Garza is a painter. Mrs. Garza is a photographer. Their seventeen-year-old daughter, Luz, is a talented writer. Their son Hugo, also seventeen, plays the violin in the school orchestra.

This Saturday, everybody is working alone. Mr. Garza is painting in the back yard. Mrs. Garza is taking photographs in the garden. Luz is writing in her bedroom, and Hugo is practicing a musical piece. He is practicing so he can get all of the notes right.

A **Now read the sentences below. Write *T* if the sentence is true, write *F* if the sentence is false, and write *?* if the story doesn't give you the information. The first two are done for you as examples.**

1. Mr. Garza is a writer.   _____F_____

2. Everyone in the Garza family is talented.   _____T_____

3. Hugo and Luz Garza also like to swim.   _____

4. Everyone is at home on Saturday.   _____

5. Mr. Garza is working in the kitchen.   _____

6. Luz is writing in the back yard.   _____

7. Mrs. Garza develops her own photographs.   _____

8. Hugo is practicing music.   _____

B **Write questions to go with the answers.**

1. _____? He is a painter.

2. _____? She is seventeen years old.

3. _____? He plays with the school orchestra.

4. _____? She is taking photographs in her garden.

5. _____? She is writing in her bedroom.

6. _____? He wants to get the notes right.

SKILL OBJECTIVES: Reviewing present form of *to be*; present progressive; forming questions. Read the story aloud and have students locate each family member in the illustration; allow time for them to reread the story silently. *Part A:* Be sure students understand the directions clearly. Do the first two together and check that the students understand why the first item is marked *F* and why the second is marked *T*. *Part B:* Go through the items orally and be sure students are phrasing questions properly before you assign the page for independent written work.

What's for Lunch?

Write sentences that describe likes and dislikes using the words in the Lunch Menu.

LUNCH MENU				
pizza	hot dogs	hamburgers	tacos	
fish	spaghetti	chop suey	chicken	lasagna
chocolate cake	apples	ice cream	grapes	

1. Carla likes tacos but she doesn't like pizza.

2. _____

3. _____

4. _____

5. _____

6. _____

7. _____

8. _____

**SKILL OBJECTIVES: Present tense; third-person singular: *likes/doesn't like.* Teach/review food vocabulary from the menu. Write and say:"I like pizza but I don't like hot dogs." Ask several students to state foods they like and dislike, then ask their classmates to recall these statements. Write the first answer on the board. *Carla likes tacos but she doesn't like pizza.* Draw attention to the forms *likes* and *doesn't like.* Do the first three items on this page orally, as a class, then assign for independent written work.

5

What Do You Like?

A Answer these questions. The first two are done for you as examples.

1. Do you like chicken? _Yes, I do. I like chicken._
2. Do you like fish? _No, I don't. I don't like fish._
3. Do you like pizza? _____
4. Do you like school? _____
5. Do you like rock music? _____

B Study the grammar in the box. Then answer the questions.

I You We They } like to sing.	He She It } likes to sing.

1. Do you like to watch TV? _Yes, I do. I like to watch TV._
2. Do you like to do your homework? _____
3. Do you like to read? _____
4. Do you like to wash the dishes? _____
5. Do you like to go shopping? _____

C Look at the pictures and answer the questions.

1. Does Lisa like to play soccer? _Yes, she does. She likes to play soccer._

2. Does Sue like to eat fish? _____
   _____

3. Does Vassily like to dance? _____
   _____

4. Do they like to clean the house? _____
   _____

5. Do they like to watch movies? _____
   _____

SKILL OBJECTIVES: Reviewing simple present tense; asking/answering questions with *do/does* ... (*like/like to*). Review the simple present tense, asking/answering questions with *do/does* ... (*like/like to*). *Parts A, B, C:* Do all items orally before assigning as independent written work. Listen for correct use of *do/does* and *don't/doesn't*. As an extension, have each student write two questions beginning, "Do you like ...?" Let a student begin the questioning, addressing any classmate he/she chooses. That classmate, after answering, may then direct one of his/her own questions to a third student.

Fannee Doolee's Secret

Language Objectives
State likes and dislikes.
Explain a pattern.

A **Fannee Doolee has a secret. She likes some things, but she doesn't like others. For example:**

> She likes spoons, but she doesn't like forks.
> She likes eggs, but she doesn't like chickens.
> She likes chess, but she doesn't like checkers.

Do you know Fannee Doolee's secret? Tell which of these things she likes and which she doesn't like.

1. _She likes_____ baseball.
2. _She doesn't like_____ magazines.
3. _____ books.
4. _____ hockey.
5. _____ tennis.
6. _____ ping pong.
7. _____ lettuce.
8. _____ puppies.
9. _____ soccer.

10. _____ to fly.
11. _____ to dance.
12. _____ to cook.
13. _____ to dress up.
14. _____ to skate.
15. _____ to wake up early.
16. _____ to kiss.
17. _____ to read.
18. _____ to hurry.

B **Carlos Gonzales also likes some things and doesn't like others.**

> He likes class, but he doesn't like school.
> He likes the Thames, but he doesn't like the Hudson.
> He likes Luis, but he doesn't like José.

Tell which things Carlos likes and which he doesn't like.

1. _He likes_____ ducks.
2. _____ paper.
3. _____ gas.
4. _____ geese.
5. _____ meat.
6. _____ pets.

Now think of some of your own.

Carlos likes _____ but he doesn't like _____.

_____ _____.

_____ _____.

_____ _____.

(*Clue:* Look at the spellings of the words. If you still aren't sure, go to page 116.)

SKILL OBJECTIVES: Classifying; deductive thinking. Read the introductory lines aloud, then assign this puzzle page for independent written work. Students who are stumped may refer to the clue written on the bottom of the page. Fannee's "secret" is at the bottom of page 116. As an extension activity, some students may enjoy creating their own secret classification and writing original "Things I Like" riddles.

7

A Chat

A **Read the following conversation.**

ED: This little blue vacuum cleaner ought to do the job, Helen.

HELEN: You always find the good ones, Ed. How much is it?

ED: Well, it seems a little expensive to me. It's $79.00.

HELEN: That isn't so bad. The big one is $98.00.

ED: Let's get the blue one, then. And then let's go around the corner to the bank.

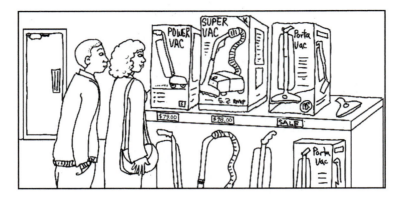

Answer the questions about the conversation. Circle the best answer. The first one is done for you.

1. Ed and Helen are

   a. shopping.   **b.** eating lunch.   **c.** at a baseball game.

2. How much does the blue vacuum cleaner cost?

   a. $92.00   **b.** $71.00   **c.** $79.00

3. How much cheaper is the little vacuum cleaner Ed likes than the big one?

   a. $50.00   **b.** $22.00   **c.** $19.00

4. Where will Ed and Helen go when they have bought the vacuum?

   a. home   **b.** across the street   **c.** around the corner

5. What does Ed want to do next?

   a. go to the bank   **b.** go to the market   **c.** go home

B **Number the sentences below to show the order of the things Ed and Helen did when they shopped for a vacuum.**

_____ They went around the corner.

_____ Ed and Helen compared the prices of two vacuums.

_____ Ed found a vacuum he liked.

_____ Ed and Helen entered the store.

_____ Ed and Helen bought the vacuum.

SKILL OBJECTIVES: **Reading for details; sequencing.** *Part A:* Have students role-play the conversation or have them read it silently. Go over any new vocabulary. To be sure the students understand the multiple-choice activity; do the first one together and discuss it. Be sure students understand that they should read all three possible answers before choosing one. *Part B:* Explain what students are to do. Have them read the sentences aloud and decide which sentence should be number 1. Then assign as independent work.

Reading a Graph

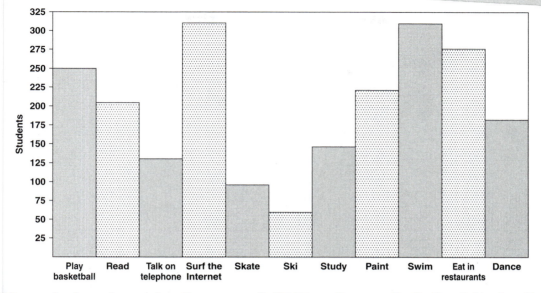

A This graph gives the results of a survey of all 325 students at the Parker School to find out what activities they like. Use the graph to decide if each of the following statements is True or False. Circle *T* if the statement is true. Circle *F* if it is false.

1. About 200 students like to surf the Internet.   T   F
2. Almost all students like to swim.   T   F
3. About 250 students like to play basketball.   T   F
4. Skiing is very popular at the Parker School.   T   F
5. More students like to paint than dance.   T   F
6. More than 100 students like to talk on the telephone.   T   F
7. About 250 students like to read.   T   F
8. About 50 students do not like to eat in restaurants.   T   F
9. More students like to dance than to read.   T   F
10. More students like to swim than to skate.   T   F
11. More than 150 students do not like to study.   T   F
12. Most students like to eat in restaurants.   T   F
13. Only 150 students like to dance.   T   F
14. Fewer than 100 students like to surf the Internet.   T   F
15. More than 200 students like to swim.   T   F

B Write about the students at the Parker School in your notebook. Begin your composition with the following topic sentence:

The students at the Parker School like to do many different things.

Be sure to indent the first line of each paragraph, to begin each sentence with a capital letter, and to end each sentence with a period.

SKILL OBJECTIVE: Interpreting a bar graph. *Part A:* Read the directions aloud. Explain any unfamiliar words. Go over the data shown on the graph. For each entry, ask: "How many students like to …?" Using a ruler will help students read the graph. Encourage students to make comparative statements about the popularity of different activities: "More students like to … than to …" Assign Part A for independent work. Correct as a class. *Part B:* Review paragraph structure, if necessary. Tell students that they can present the information in any order they wish. Assign for independent written work.

What's Wrong?

Language Objectives
Talk about inaccuracies in a picture prompt. Write about inaccuracies.

A **Study the picture. Can you find ten problems? Write them below. Find the words in the Data Bank. The first one is done for you.**

1. _A man is eating a shoe._
2. _____
3. _____
4. _____
5. _____
6. _____
7. _____
8. _____
9. _____
10. _____

DATA BANK

eating	drinking	wearing	playing	sleeping	reading	taking

B **Now, in paragraph form, describe what is happening in the restaurant. The topic sentence introduces the story.**

Today is a crazy day at Ron's Restaurant. _____

_____

_____

_____

_____

_____

_____

SKILL OBJECTIVES: Reviewing the present progressive; writing a paragraph from a picture. *Part A:* Have students discuss the picture and complete the ten items individually or in pairs. You may want to discuss why the items they have written are "problems" or "wrong." *Part B:* Explain *topic sentence, concluding sentence,* and *format.* Then have students use the ten sentences from Part A to form a paragraph. Call attention to the fact that the first line is indented; remind students to use proper punctuation and capitalization.

Helping You Study: the Table of Contents

Language Objective
Answer questions about a table of contents.

The Table of Contents in a book is an important help to you in studying. The Table of Contents is a list of the chapters or units in the book. It tells you the name of the chapter and the page number for the first page of the chapter. Here is a sample Table of Contents from a beginner's book in English as a Second Language. Look at the Table of Contents and then answer the questions about it.

Table of Contents

Chapter 1   Say Hello! 3

Chapter 2   The Clothes You Wear 12

Chapter 3   The Jobs You Do 25

Chapter 4   The Foods You Eat 36

Chapter 5   The People in Your Family 44

Chapter 6   The Rooms in Your House 57

Chapter 7   The Days of the Week and the Months of the Year 69

Chapter 8   The Weather 81

Chapter 9   The Places You Go 86

Chapter 10   The Machines You Use 90

Chapter 11   The Sports and Games You Play 108

Chapter 12   The Parts of the Body 112

Answer the questions. Use the Table of Contents to help you. The first one is done for you.

1. What chapter tells about meat, fruit, and vegetables? _____4_____

2. What chapter tells about hats, coats, and dresses? _____

3. What chapter tells about brothers, sisters, and cousins? _____

4. What chapter tells about January, February, and March? _____

5. What chapter tells about feet, hands, and legs? _____

6. What chapter tells about rain, wind, and sun? _____

7. What chapter tells about the kitchen, living room, and dining room? _____

8. What chapter tells about school, the library, and the museum? _____

9. What chapter tells about football, baseball, and checkers? _____

10. What page is the first page of Chapter 5? _____

11. What page is the first page of Chapter 7? _____

12. What page is the first page of Chapter 11? _____

13. What page is the last page of Chapter 8? _____

14. What page is the last page of Chapter 3? _____

SKILL OBJECTIVES: Using a Table of Contents; interpreting chapter titles. Go over the introductory paragraph and sample Table of Contents with the class. Answer some or all of the questions with the class before assigning the page as independent written work. As an extension activity, have students locate, examine, and ask each other questions about the Tables of Contents in several textbooks they are using.

Dear Dot

Dear Dot,

I have three older brothers—Ricky, Paul, and Sammy. I wear Ricky's old clothes. I use Paul's old bike, and I have Sammy's teacher in school this year. I want some new things, some things that belong only to me. I'm tired of hand-me-downs. What can I do?

Second-Hand Roberto

1. How many brothers does Roberto have? _____

2. Whose clothes does Roberto wear? _____

3. Whose bike does he use? _____

4. Whose teacher does he have? _____

5. What does Roberto want? _____

6. What does the phrase *hand-me-downs* in this letter mean? Circle the best answer.

    a. new things   **b.** broken things   **c.** used things   **d.** hungry people

7. What is your advice to Roberto? Write a short answer. _____

    _____

    _____

8. Now read Dot's answer. See if your answer is the same. If your answer is different, tell why you disagree.

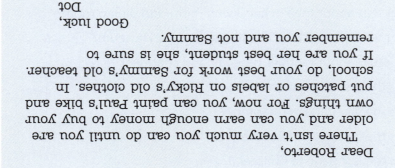

Dear Roberto,

There isn't very much you can do until you are older and you can earn enough money to buy your own things. For now, you can paint Paul's bike and put patches or labels on Ricky's old clothes. In school, do your best work for Sammy's old teacher. If you are her best student, she is sure to remember you and not Sammy.

Good luck,
Dot

SKILL OBJECTIVES: Reading comprehension; understanding words through context; making judgments. "Dear Dot" letters appear periodically throughout this book. Each letter presents a creative problem-solving situation that should generate lively classroom discussion. Students should be encouraged to defend their own opinions, as well as be open to others' advice. Read the letter aloud. Explain new words. Have students reread the letter silently, then complete the questions. Correct and discuss as a class.

Unit 2 — What Do They Do?

Careers and Activities

Language Objective
Describe career activities using the third-person singular present tense.

A Look at the pictures. Write the name of the occupation. Then write what the people do. The first one is done for you.

1. _He is a mail carrier._   _He delivers mail._

2. _____   _____

3. _____   _____

4. _____   _____

5. _____   _____

6. _____   _____

B Circle the best answer. Then write the answer in the blank.

1. A tailor _____.
   a. teaches
   b. types
   c. sews

2. A teller _____.
   a. cashes checks
   b. delivers mail
   c. drives a taxi

3. A pilot _____.
   a. takes pictures
   b. works in a bank
   c. flies planes

4. A waitress _____.
   a. cooks food
   b. serves food
   c. drives a bus

5. A hairdresser _____.
   a. fixes cars
   b. cuts hair
   c. sells shoes

6. A construction worker _____.
   a. cleans buildings
   b. builds buildings
   c. designs buildings

7. An astronaut _____.
   a. travels in space
   b. fixes planes
   c. directs traffic

8. An electrician _____.
   a. installs wiring
   b. fixes sinks
   c. cleans teeth

SKILL OBJECTIVES: Reviewing the simple present tense; building vocabulary. *Part A:* Discuss the pictures and go through the six items orally. Be sure students pronounce the *-s* in the third person singular. Then assign for independent written work. *Part B:* Review vocabulary as necessary. Do the first three or four items as a group, then assign as independent work.

What Do You Want to Be?

A Write a sentence that tells what each one wants to be, using words from the Data Bank. Use the plural form, if necessary. The first one is done for you.

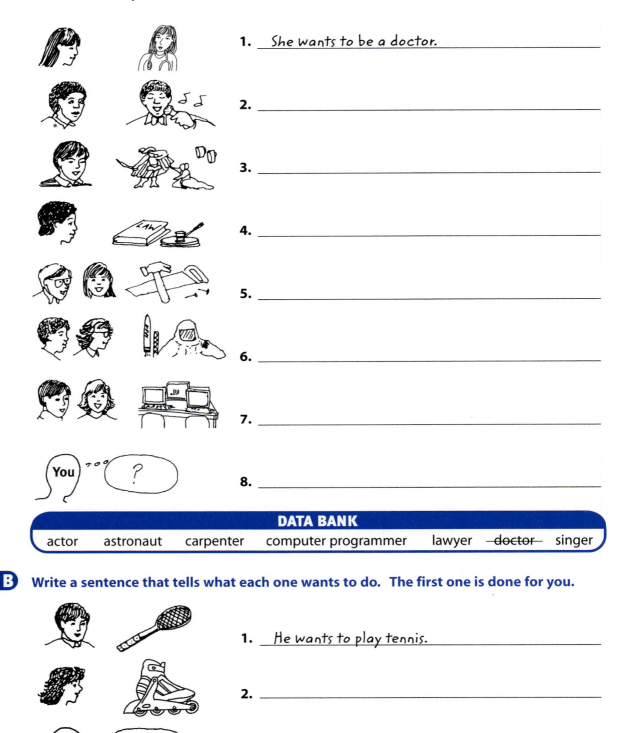

1. She wants to be a doctor.

2. _____

3. _____

4. _____

5. _____

6. _____

7. _____

8. _____

DATA BANK

actor   astronaut   carpenter   computer programmer   lawyer   ~~doctor~~   singer

B Write a sentence that tells what each one wants to do. The first one is done for you.

1. He wants to play tennis.

2. _____

3. _____

SKILL OBJECTIVE: Present tense: *want(s) to.* Teach/review the occupation titles in the Data Bank. Then help students list as many other occupations as they can. Ask various students, "What do you want to be?" *Part A:* Have students offer sentences orally. Listen for correct use of *want/wants.* Assign for independent written work. *Part B:* Ask several students: "What do you want to do after school today?" Then ask classmates to recall these statements. "What does (Carlos) want to do?" Again, listen for correct use of *want/wants.* Assign for independent work.

14

Choosing a Career

Read the stories.

I'm George. I like to help sick animals. I want to be a veterinarian. I have to take a college preparatory course in high school, and I have to attend college for four years. After that, I have to attend a college of veterinary medicine for four years.

Claudia and Armando like to play computer games, and they like to use the computers in their high school. They want to design computer software. In high school, they have to take a college course. Then they have to attend college. Many colleges now offer computer courses.

Binh and Dao like to fix old cars. They want to be mechanics. They have to take a general course in high school or go to a vocational-technical school. They don't have to go to college.

Hiro also likes computers. He wants to be a computer programmer. He is taking computer programming in high school. He will then go to a two-year college where he'll study computer programming.

We like to help people. We want to be police officers. We have to be high school graduates, and we have to study for a civil service exam. When we pass the exam, we can apply for jobs. Town or city officials appoint police officers. We can go to college for two years if we want to get an associate's degree in law enforcement.

My name is Vanya. I am also interested in helping people. I would like to work in a doctor's office. I have to go to a business school for two years after high school, so it's a good idea to take the college preparatory course in high school. In business school, I plan to learn medical terminology. I also plan to learn how to use a computer.

A How about you? Write about what you want to do. Tell about the education you will need.

_____

_____

_____

B Now look at the following sentences. If a sentence is true, circle *T*. If it is false, circle *F*.

1. You have to go to college to become a mechanic.   T   F

2. You have to go to college to become a computer programmer.   T   F

3. You have to take a civil service exam to become a police officer.   T   F

4. You have to attend college for eight years to become a veterinarian.   T   F

5. A mechanic can get training in a vocational-technical school.   T   F

6. You have to attend college for four years to work in a doctor's office.   T   F

SKILL OBJECTIVES: Using *like(s) to, want(s) to, has/have to*; reading for details; writing a paragraph. Read the paragraphs aloud. Explain any unfamiliar vocabulary. Allow time for students to reread silently. Have several students tell what they like to do and what they would like to do for a career. Let the class discuss the education needed. Let students complete this page independently. Correct the true/false questions together, then have volunteers read their paragraphs to the class.

What's Their Job?

Language Objectives
Name careers from context clues. Write about the daily activities of a teacher.

A | Use the words in Data Bank A to complete each statement.

1. I can repair engines, install mufflers, change tires, and fix brakes.

   I am a _____.

2. I take photographs and later develop them. Newspapers publish my photographs.

   I am a _____.

3. I work in a department store. I help people find what they want. I use the cash register and give people receipts.

   I am a _____.

4. I help people make wills. I write contracts. I help people who have to go to court. I help people get money that others owe them.

   I am a _____.

5. I can use an adding machine and a computer. I work with payrolls and send out paychecks.

   I am a _____.

6. I help sick animals. People come to my office with their animals for regular checkups.

   I am a _____.

DATA BANK A

| bookkeeper | lawyer | veterinarian | mechanic | photographer | sales clerk |

B | Here are some short paragraphs about different people. Put a title on each paragraph. Use Data Bank B for your titles. The first one is done for you.

1. _The Doctor_ — She works in a hospital. She operates on sick people. She helps her patients. She knows a lot about medicine.

2. _____ — He works at a radio station. He plays music. He interviews musicians. He entertains people who listen.

3. _____ — She works in a hotel. She cleans up. She washes and polishes. She makes beds.

4. _____ — He works in a supermarket. He rings up the prices of food at his register. He packs the bags. He helps his customers.

DATA BANK B

| The Disc Jockey | The Maid | ~~The Doctor~~ | The Cashier |

C | Write a paragraph like the ones above about "The Teacher."

_____

_____

_____

_____

_____

SKILL OBJECTIVES: Identifying topics; building vocabulary; drawing conclusions; writing a paragraph. *Part A:* Have students look at Data Bank A first to see how many occupations they already know. Have them explain them in their own words. Help with pronunciation, if necessary. Have students do the first item as a group to be sure they understand the directions. Then assign as independent written work. *Part B:* Follow the same procedure. *Part C:* Have students write a paragraph, similar to those in Part B, item 2, about "The Teacher." Before they write, discuss the various responsibilities of a teacher, writing them on the board as they are mentioned.

What, Where, and Why?

The present progressive tense uses the verb *to be* and an *-ing* word.

Examples: I am talking.   You are calling.   He is asking.

   We are eating.   They are driving.

A **Use the present progressive tense to help you answer each of the questions. The first one is done for you.**

1. What is the mail carrier doing?

   He (deliver) _____ *is delivering* _____ the mail.

2. What are the astronauts doing now?

   They (travel) _____ in space.

3. Is the pilot talking to the passengers?

   No, he (fly) _____ the plane.

4. What is the bank teller doing?

   She (cash) _____ a check.

5. Where's the waiter?

   He (serve) _____ food in the dining room.

6. Why are the photographers outside?

   They (take) _____ photographs of a movie star.

7. Are the sales clerks busy?

   No, they (stand) _____ in the aisles talking.

B **Use the present progressive tense to complete the following sentences. The first one is done for you.**

1. The actors (learn) _____ *are learning* _____ their lines.

2. The lawyer (talk) _____ to the judge.

3. The carpenters (make) _____ a table.

4. The police officer (stop) _____ the traffic.

5. You (do) _____ a good job at the store.

6. Ivan (take) _____ classes in computer programming.

7. The singer (practice) _____ her new song.

SKILL OBJECTIVE: Reviewing the present progressive tense. Discuss the present progressive tense. Read the explanatory box to the students and review the present tense of *to be*. *Part A:* Do the first two items orally with the students; be sure students use the correct form of *to be*. *Part B:* Again check to be sure that students use the correct form of *to be*—that they equate "The actors" with "They" and "The lawyer" with "He" or "She." Then assign for independent written work.

Present or Present Progressive?

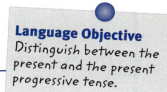

Language Objective
Distinguish between the present and the present progressive tense.

The present tense shows actions that happen repeatedly or *every day*. The present progressive tense shows actions that are happening *now*. Look at the following examples.

Present	Present Progressive
A mail carrier delivers the mail every day. A teller cashes checks at a bank. An electrician installs wiring.	The mail carrier is delivering the mail now. The teller is cashing my check now. The electrician is installing the wiring now.

Complete each sentence with the correct tense.

1. The astronauts _____ in space now.
   are traveling / travel

2. The pilot _____ to Brazil every Monday.
   is flying / flies

3. The waitresses _____ breakfast at the restaurant every morning.
   are serving / serve

4. The hairdresser _____ hair every day.
   is cutting / cuts

5. The office assistant _____ the letter now.
   is typing / types

6. The carpenters _____ our house now.
   are building / build

7. A veterinarian _____ animals.
   is taking care of / takes care of

8. The police officer _____ the robber now.
   is arresting / arrests

9. The sales clerks _____ a lot of fans every summer.
   are selling / sell

10. Doctors _____ their patients.
    are helping / help

11. The hairdresser is busy now; he _____ a customer's hair.
    is cutting / cuts

12. Disc jockeys _____ songs on the radio.
    are playing / play

SKILL OBJECTIVE: Contrasting the present tenses. Discuss the grammar box and the examples; ask students for additional examples. The distinction between the tenses is difficult for many students to make. Do the entire page orally if students need the practice in either the grammar or pronunciation; then assign as independent written work.

Helping You Study: Alphabetical Order (1)

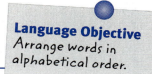

Language Objective
Arrange words in alphabetical order.

A useful way of listing words is in alphabetical order. This means the order in which the words' first letters appear in the alphabet. For example, here is a list of words in alphabetical order:

apple   dinner   fly   jump   marry

Apple is first because its first letter, *a*, is the first letter in the alphabet. *Dinner* is next because its first letter, *d*, comes in the alphabet before the first letters of the other words. And so on.

A Here are four lists of words that you know. Rewrite each list in alphabetical order. The first two words are done for you.

pig	_antelope_	teacher	_____
sheep	_cat_	plumber	_____
cat	_____	jeweler	_____
dog	_____	carpenter	_____
antelope	_____	farmer	_____

rice	_____	tennis	_____
tomato	_____	soccer	_____
chicken	_____	baseball	_____
fish	_____	hockey	_____
beans	_____	football	_____

B When the words begin with the same letter, use the second letter to alphabetize. Rewrite each list in alphabetical order. The first two words are done for you.

sweater	_shirt_	carrots	_____
shirt	_sleeve_	cheese	_____
socks	_____	celery	_____
sneakers	_____	cupcake	_____
sleeve	_____	cream	_____

DATA BANK

A B C D E F G H I J K L M N O P Q R S T U V W X Y Z

SKILL OBJECTIVE: Alphabetizing by first and second letters. Read the explanatory paragraphs aloud. Then write the first names of five students on the board. Help the class alphabetize the list. Repeat this activity if students need more practice. Read the instructions for Part B aloud, then write the days of the week on the board. Help the class alphabetize these seven words. When students seem comfortable with this skill, assign the page for independent written work. *Extension Activity:* Have students name the category represented by each word list.

Helping You Study: Alphabetical Order (2)

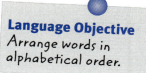

A When words start with the same two letters, you have to use the third letter to put them in alphabetical order. Write each of these lists in alphabetical order.

cheese   _____

chocolate   _____

change   _____

church   _____

chicken   _____

spoon   _____

spring   _____

speak   _____

splash   _____

spy   _____

B Now try these long columns. Be careful. Sometimes you are going to have to use second, third, or even fourth letters.

Column A

dog   _____

purple   _____

floor   _____

square   _____

black   _____

make   _____

armchair   _____

man   _____

swim   _____

gloves   _____

pilot   _____

uncle   _____

blast   _____

warm   _____

blond   _____

jacket   _____

Column B

museum   _____

read   _____

not   _____

sister   _____

last   _____

parts   _____

snow   _____

now   _____

quarter   _____

throat   _____

late   _____

rug   _____

parents   _____

thumb   _____

lawyer   _____

pants   _____

SKILL OBJECTIVE: Alphabetizing. Read the directions to Part A aloud. If you wish, have a volunteer write the alphabet on the board for student reference. Alphabetize the first column of words as a class. Assign the rest of the page for independent written work. For additional practice in this skill, write the names of the months on the board and have students alphabetize these twelve words.

Dear Dot

Dear Dot

Dear Dot,

My boyfriend, Dennis, likes cars. He reads about cars, talks about cars, thinks about cars, and probably dreams about them too. He wants to be a mechanic when he finishes school. All of that is okay with me, but there is one problem. Dennis drives too fast. He thinks that he knows everything about cars, and that nothing can happen to us. I know we are going to have an accident soon. Sometimes he drives over eighty miles an hour. What can I do?

Nervous

1. What does Dennis like? _____

2. What does Dennis want to be? _____

3. What is Nervous's problem? _____

_____

4. Why does Dennis drive fast _____

_____

5. What does the word *accident* in this letter mean? Circle the best answer.

    a. mistake   **b.** crash   **c.** murder   **d.** problem

6. What is your advice to Nervous? Write a short answer. _____

_____

7. Now read Dot's answer. See if your answer is the same. If your answer is different, tell why you disagree. Dot's advice is below.

Dear Nervous,

You should stay out of Dennis's car. More than 6,000 teenagers die every year in car accidents in the United States. They die because too many teenagers drive too fast, and drive after drinking alcohol. You have to protect yourself. Tell your boyfriend you are not going to ride with him until he slows down. And when you do start to ride with him, remember to wear your seat belt!

Dot

SKILL OBJECTIVES: Reading comprehension; understanding words through context; making judgments. Read the letter aloud to the class, then have them reread it silently. Have students answer questions 1–6. Correct the first five questions as a class. Encourage discussion of question 6, then have students write their answers to it. Have them read Dot's answer and discuss how it agrees and disagrees with their own advice to Nervous.

21

Unit **3** A Day in the Life of Ernest

Always, Sometimes, Never

There are some things Ernest always does. There are other things Ernest never does. And Ernest does other things some of the time. Read this chart to find out how often Ernest does the things he does.

How Often

	Always	Often	Sometimes	Seldom	Never
1. Works in the garden					X
2. Listens to CDs		X			
3. Watches TV			X		
4. Makes a salad			X		
5. Builds model ships				X	
6. Reads science fiction		X			
7. Goes hiking				X	
8. Goes swimming				X	
9. Plays soccer with friends			X		
10. Eats cereal for breakfast	X				
11. Goes to the zoo					X
12. Eats sandwiches		X			

Write sentences telling how often Ernest does each thing on the list. Use the chart. The first sentence is done for you.

1. _Ernest never works in the garden._
2. _____
3. _____
4. _____
5. _____
6. _____
7. _____
8. _____
9. _____
10. _____
11. _____
12. _____

Odd Man Out

A **Circle the word that doesn't belong.** **The first one is done for you.**

1. bus   train   (house)   plane
2. potato   lamb   pork   beef
3. soccer   basketball   football   checkers
4. drum   window   piano   flute
5. comic book   newspaper   ball   magazine
6. fish   coffee   milk   lemonade
7. sweater   pants   gloves   door
8. pineapple   lettuce   orange   banana
9. sofa   table   kitchen   chair
10. roast beef breakfast   lunch   dinner
11. November   December   July   Sunday
12. teeth   men   children   foot
13. eyes   hands   nose   mouth
14. cup   hammer   saw   pliers
15. Chinese   French   English   United States

B **Read each statement. Decide if it is about something that happens *always*, or *often*, or *seldom*, or *never*. Then write one of these words next to each statement: *always, often, seldom, never*. The first one is done for you.**

1. Dogs speak English.   _____*never*_____
2. The sun rises in the east.   _____
3. People walk on the moon.   _____
4. Money grows on trees.   _____
5. Spaceships from Mars visit the Earth.   _____
6. Drunken drivers cause accidents on the roads.   _____

C **Write a sentence of your own for each one of these words.**

(always) _____

(often)   _____

(seldom) _____

(never)   _____

SKILL OBJECTIVES: Classifying; using adverbs of frequency. Do several examples in each part as a class, then let students complete the page independently. Correct and discuss the answers together. For Part A, let students explain why three of the words are alike, and why the fourth word does not belong. Correct Part B as a class. Let each student read his/her favorite sentence from Part C.

Life in a Fire Station

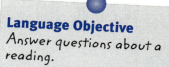

Read the story.

A fire station can be a challenging but rewarding place to work. The men and women who work there are called firefighters.

Firefighters learn about a fire when a dispatch center contacts them. When someone calls 911 to report a fire, the call is answered by someone at the dispatch center. That person calls the fire station nearest the fire.

When a call is received at a fire station, the firefighters leave to fight the fire immediately. They must always be ready to do their job at short notice. The number of firefighters sent depends on the size of the fire. A two-alarm fire means that firefighters from another station, or additional equipment, are needed to help put the fire out. Three-, four-, and five-alarm fires require even more help.

Fighting fires is a very risky job. It requires courage and teamwork. The men and women battling a fire have to cooperate with each other.

When they are not fighting fires, firefighters may do many things. Some of them may go to schools to talk to students about their jobs and about how to prevent fires in homes. Some may clean the fire station and the firefighting equipment. Others may train new recruits so that they can do their job more effectively.

A Now answer the questions. Use complete sentences. The first one is done for you.

1. How do firefighters find out about fires? _They find out about them from_
   dispatch centers.

2. What number is called if there is a fire or another emergency? _____

3. What decides how many firefighters go to fight a fire? _____

   _____

4. What are two things that firefighting requires? _____

   _____

5. What are some other things firefighters do? _____

   _____

6. What do the firefighters do to their equipment when they are not using it? _____

   _____

7. Why do firefighters train new recruits while they are not fighting fires? _____

   _____

B What is the story mostly about? Circle the best answer.

a. fires   **b.** firefighting equipment   **c.** the firefighter's job   **d.** 911

SKILL OBJECTIVES: Identifying main idea and details; understanding adverbs of frequency. Read the story aloud. Explain any unfamiliar vocabulary. Let students discuss experiences they have had with firefighters. Ask students to reread the story silently. You may wish to cover a few questions as a group before assigning the page as independent written work. Correct and discuss the answers together. Encourage volunteers to explain why "the firefighter's job" is the correct answer to Part B.

Depositing a Check

Read the story.

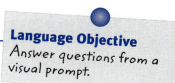

Lee Meng is thirteen years old. He delivers papers each morning before school. He doesn't like getting up early. But he likes earning money.

Every week Lee gets a check from his boss. This is his payment.

He deposits his paycheck in his savings account. Then he withdraws some money each week to spend.

The person or company who is receiving the check

How much check is for (in words)

The bank's number

The Daily Mirror's checking account number

The Daily Mirror **122 Spruce Street** **Dale, VA 00567**	**No.** 314
	February 10, 2005 **Date**
Pay to the order of Lee Meng	**$ 50.00**
Fifty Dollars	**Dollars** Security Features Included. Details on Back.
Dale City Bank **Virginia**	
For	*Carla Lambert* **Carla Lambert, Vice President**
[: 566483099]: 655 774 556 233	

Number of check

How much the check is for (in numbers)

Signature

1. What is the check number? _____ What is the date of the check? _____

2. Why do you think the amount of the check is written twice, in numbers and in words?

   _____

3. What is the name of the company paying the check? _____

4. How much is the check for? _____

5. What is Lee Meng's account number? _____

A **To deposit the check, Lee must endorse it. That means he must sign his name on the back of it. Then the check goes into his savings account. Lee always deposits his check at a bank. After a few days, the bank's records show that Lee's account has increased.**

1. Why do you think Lee has to endorse the check to deposit it? _____

   _____

2. Why do you think it takes a few days for the bank's records to show that Lee has made a

   deposit? _____

   _____

SKILL OBJECTIVES: Reading a check; understanding bank procedures. Read the introductory paragraphs aloud. Let the class discuss the questions posed at the end. How many students have received checks? What did they do with them? How many have checking accounts? *Part A:* Examine the check as a class. Let students answer the questions orally. *Part B:* Allow time for students to answer these questions independently. Then have the class compare answers and discuss the problems.

Opening a Savings Account

Read the story.

Lee Meng has put some of the money he makes from his paper route into a savings account. The bank pays interest to Lee for using his money in the account. This interest is added to his account each month.

If you want to open your own savings account, first you have to complete a signature card. There are spaces on the card for your name, address, and social security number. On some cards, you may have to write the last name your mother had before she got married. The bank asks for this information in case someone else tries to take money out of your account.

You will get an Automatic Teller Machine (ATM) card with the account. When you put this card in an ATM machine and type in a special code you get at the bank, you can take money out of your account.

A When you open a savings account, the bank keeps a record of it. The bank's computer keeps a record that shows when you put money into the account or take money out of it. The computer also keeps track of the interest the account earns. This is part of a report on Lee's account. Use it to answer the questions.

Date	Deposit	Withdrawal	Interest	Balance
4/1/05	50.00	30.00		486.25
4/8/05	50.00	10.00		526.25
4/15/05	50.00	20.00		556.25
4/22/05	50.00	20.00		586.25
4/29/05	50.00	25.00	2%	623.48
5/6/05	50.00	20.00		653.48

1. How much money does Lee Meng earn each week? _____
2. How much interest does Lee earn on April 29? _____
3. How much money has Lee saved between April 1 and May 6? _____
4. How much money does Lee take out on April 8? _____

B Here is a signature card to open a savings account. Fill it out using the following information.

Lee Meng was born on March 13, 1988. His social security number is 001-67-3554. He lives on 9 Cherry Lane, in Lubbock, Texas. His zip code is 78009. His phone number is 703-555-5677. His mother's name was Wei Lin.

	The undersigned hereby agree to the by-laws of the DALE CITY BANK relating to savings deposits now or hereafter in force and agree(s) to the regulations governing the use of this account and acknowledge(s) receipt of a copy of said regulations.
No.	

☐ SINGLE ACCOUNT ☐ JOINT ACCOUNT

#1 Sign here	#2 Sign here
Print name here	Print name here
Social Security number	Social Security number
Telephone number	Telephone number
Number Street Apt #	Number Street Apt #
City, State, Zip code	City, State, Zip code
Date of birth	Date of birth
Mother's maiden name	Mother's maiden name
For bank use only-ID	For bank use only-ID
DATE OPENED BY	DATE OPENED BY

SKILL OBJECTIVES: Learning about savings accounts; understanding entries in a statement. Read the introductory paragraphs aloud. Discuss unfamiliar vocabulary and concepts. *Part A:* Examine the statement together. Have students practice reading the dates and describing the activity that took place in the account on that day. *Part B:* Discuss what a joint account is and provide help as needed; students will fill out only the left part of the signature card. Correct and discuss answers with the class.

A Student Survey

This chart shows the results of a survey of 100 students asking how often they do different things. The numbers on the chart show how many students do each thing never, sometimes, usually, often, or always.

Number of Students

	Never	Sometimes	Usually	Often	Always
Help your mother	2	16	25	30	27
Wash the dishes	22	20	20	15	23
Empty the trash	12	30	15	18	25
Make your bed	5	26	20	36	13
Do your homework	2	19	30	30	19
Get up at 5:30 a.m.	89	10	1	0	0
Buy school lunch	24	14	26	26	10
Read school newspapers	3	30	20	20	27
Speak English at home	12	20	5	5	58
Cook your own supper	44	10	21	15	10

Use the chart to answer the questions. The first one is done for you.

1. How many students usually do their homework? _____30 usually do.____
2. How many students never wash the dishes? _____
3. How many students always make their beds? _____
4. How many students sometimes buy school lunches? _____
5. How many students usually get up at 5:30 a.m.? _____
6. How many students often empty the trash? _____
7. How many students always speak English at home? _____
8. How many students never read school newspapers? _____
9. How many students usually cook their own supper? _____
10. How many students sometimes help their mother? _____
11. How many students always get up at 5:30 a.m.? _____
12. How many students never do their homework? _____
13. How many students usually speak English at home? _____
14. How many students never empty the trash? _____

SKILL OBJECTIVES: Interpreting a chart; using adverbs of frequency. Ask questions about the information on this chart, first having students refer to each statistic in order ("How many students never/sometimes/often … help their mother?"), then having them use the grid to locate scattered information. ("How many students usually buy lunch/never get up at 5:30 a.m. etc.?") Let students ask each other questions. Assign the page for independent written work. Students can use this chart as a questionnaire form for their own class. They can then tabulate and report the results.

Is That a Fact?

Here are some statements about Thanksgiving. Decide if each is a fact or an opinion. Remember that facts are true statements that you can read or check in an encyclopedia or other reference book. Opinions are what a person thinks or feels about something. They are true for the person, but they may not be true for other people.

Read each statement. Write *Fact* if the statement is a fact. Write *Opinion* if it is an opinion.

1. Turkey is no good without gravy. _____

2. Thanksgiving is a holiday in the United States. _____

3. There is a big parade in New York City on Thanksgiving Day. _____

4. Thanksgiving is the fourth Thursday in November. _____

5. It's nice to be with family on a holiday. _____

6. It is an American tradition to eat turkey on Thanksgiving. _____

7. Thanksgiving is the best holiday of the year. _____

8. Thanksgiving is an autumn (fall) holiday. _____

9. President Lincoln declared Thanksgiving a holiday in 1863. _____

10. Apple pie and ice cream is a delicious dessert. _____

11. The only good vegetables are broccoli and pumpkin. _____

12. Apple cider is the traditional Thanksgiving drink. _____

13. Apple cider isn't good; it's too sweet. _____

14. Banks, post offices, and schools are closed on Thanksgiving. _____

15. Thanksgiving dinners are a lot of work and trouble. _____

16. Thanksgiving is a happy day. _____

17. The next holiday after Thanksgiving is Christmas. _____

18. Everyone eats too much on Thanksgiving. _____

19. A turkey dinner is a delicious meal. _____

20. The Pilgrims celebrated their first Thanksgiving in 1621. _____

SKILL OBJECTIVE: Distinguishing between fact and opinion. Read and discuss the explanation on the top of the page. All the facts and opinions in this activity refer to Thanksgiving. Let the students briefly discuss what they know about this holiday. Complete and discuss several examples on this page as a class. Be sure students understand that none of the sentences are false. When students are secure with the concept, assign the page for independent work. Correct and discuss as a class.

Have or Has?

A Fill in the blanks with *have* or *has*. Use the following rule.

| I
You
We
They | } have | | He
She
It | } has |

1. How are you today?
   Terrible. I _____ a headache.

2. How is Lisa?
   Terrible. She _____ an earache.

3. How is Jim?
   Terrible. He _____ a bad cold.

4. How are they?
   Terrible. They _____ the flu.

5. How is your dog?
   Terrible. It _____ a broken leg.

6. How are you?
   Terrible. I _____ a stomachache.

B Read the following story about the Ruiz family. Then answer the questions by writing *Yes* or *No*.

   This is the Ruiz family. Mr. and Mrs. Ruiz have three children, Lisa, Rosa, and Roberto, and two pets, a dog and a cat. In the summer, the children always have fun together at the beach. They seldom have trouble finding friends to go with them. Lisa never has enough time for all the things she wants to do. Mrs. Ruiz usually has dinner waiting when they get home. In the evening, Rosa often has a date with one of her boyfriends, and Roberto sometimes has a chess game with his mother.

1. Do Mr. and Mrs. Ruiz have two children? _____

2. Do Mr. and Mrs. Ruiz have two pets? _____

3. Do the Ruiz children have a good time together? _____

4. Do they have trouble finding friends? _____

5. Does Lisa usually have enough time? _____

6. Does Rosa have more than one boyfriend? _____

7. Does Lisa usually have dinner waiting? _____

8. Does Mrs. Ruiz know how to play chess? _____

C Complete the following sentences with *have* or *has*.

1. Ricardo _____ a new car.

2. Maria _____ brown eyes.

3. We _____ many friends in Miami.

4. My dog _____ a short tail.

5. The house _____ eight rooms.

6. Tom and Helen _____ red hair.

7. She and I _____ fun in school.

8. César _____ a bad temper.

SKILL OBJECTIVES: Present forms of *to have*; reading for details. Review the verb chart at the top of the page. Go over the directions for all three parts. You may wish to do one or more examples as a class, before assigning the page for independent work.

29

Helping You Study: Using the Dictionary (1)

The words in a dictionary are in alphabetical order. You know that words that begin with the letter *c*, for example, come after words that begin with the letter *b*, and that words that begin with *w* come after words that begin with *u* or *v*.

But you don't have to go through all the pages before the words that begin with *w* to look up the word, *waver,* for example. You need only look in the right section of the dictionary.

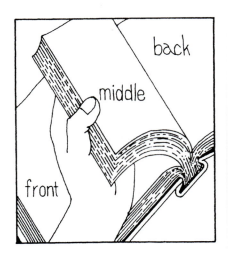

Look in the **front** section of the dictionary for words that begin with A, B, C, D, E, F, and G.

Look in the **middle** section of the dictionary for words that begin with H, I, J, K, L, M, N, O, and P.

Look in the **back** section of the dictionary for words that begin with Q, R, S, T, U, V, W, X, Y, and Z.

A Tell what section of the dictionary these words are in. The first one is done for you.

1. tomorrow _back_	8. tooth _____	15. executive _____
2. please _____	9. architect _____	16. yellow _____
3. elbow _____	10. kitchen _____	17. jacket _____
4. bad _____	11. wet _____	18. concert _____
5. green _____	12. store _____	19. middle _____
6. office _____	13. beans _____	20. train _____
7. window _____	14. hair _____	21. island _____

B Answer the questions. Write *before* or *after*.

1. Is *ape* before or after *zebra* in the dictionary? _____

2. Is *kitchen* before or after *cook* in the dictionary? _____

3. Is *milk* before or after *cow* in the dictionary? _____

4. Is *top* before or after *bottom* in the dictionary? _____

5. Is *chicken* before or after *egg* in the dictionary? _____

SKILL OBJECTIVE: Approximating the location of a word in the dictionary. Read the explanatory sentences at the top of the page aloud. Do a number of examples from Parts A and B as a group, then assign the page as independent written work. Correct as a class. As an extension activity, provide students with dictionaries and organize a dictionary race. Hold up a word on a flashcard. The first student to find the word must read the definition aloud. Score can be kept by giving points to individuals or to teams.

Dear Dot

Dear Dot

Dear Dot,
   I am the only girl in my family. I have four brothers. I almost always do the dishes and wash the clothes. My mother works, so I often do the cooking, too. My brothers almost never help clean the house, and they always mess it up. I am tired of doing all the work in the house. What can I do?

                                                        Cinderella

1. How many children are in Cinderella's family? _____

2. What does she almost always do? _____

3. Why does she do the cooking? _____

4. What do her brothers almost never do? _____

5. What does the phrase *mess up* in this letter mean? Circle the best answer.

   a. make dirty   **b.** make clean   **c.** destroy   **d.** help

6. What is your advice for Cinderella? Write a short answer. _____

   _____

   _____

7. Now read Dot's answer. See if your answer is the same. If your answer is different, tell why you disagree. Dot's advice is below.

Dear Cinderella,
   You need some help. You have to have a family meeting. Talk to your mother and your brothers. Tell them how much work you are doing and how little work your brothers are doing. Make a chart or write a list of things to do and give everyone a job. Ask your mother to check to see who is and who isn't doing their job. You don't have to do all the work in your house. Your brothers should help you.
                                    Good luck,
                                    Dot

SKILL OBJECTIVES: Reading comprehension; understanding words through context; making judgments. Read the letter aloud as students follow along. Define any unfamiliar words. Explain the fairy tale character, Cinderella. Ask students if a similar story is told in their native country. Ask, "Why does this letter writer sign herself, Cinderella?" Have students reread the letter silently, then answer the questions. Correct answers as a class. Have students compare and discuss their own advice and Dot's reply. Encourage lively discussion.

Dr. Schwartz's Schedule

Dr. Schwartz is a busy veterinarian. Here is his schedule.

7:45	He leaves for work.
8:00	He gets to his office; reviews records.
9:00	He begins seeing patients.
12:00	He goes to lunch.
1:00	He comes back from lunch; sees more patients.
5:30	He leaves his office.
5:45	He has dinner at a restaurant.
7:30	He teaches at City College twice a week.
8:30	He leaves for home.

Read Dr. Schwartz's daily schedule. Then write questions about him. The answer to each question is at the right. The question you write has to go with this answer. The first word or words of each question are at the left. The first question is done for you.

1. When <u>*does he leave for work?*</u>   He leaves for work at 7:45.

2. How long _____? It takes him 15 minutes.

3. When _____? He arrives at 8:00.

4. What _____? He gets to his office and reviews records.

5. How long _____? For one hour.

6. When _____? He goes at 12:00.

7. What _____? He comes back to work and sees more patients.

8. How long _____? He sees patients for four and a half hours.

9. Why _____? He is finished working for the day.

10. When _____? At 5:45.

11. Where _____? He has dinner at a restaurant.

12. Does _____? No, he goes to City College.

13. What _____? He teaches a class twice a week.

14. When _____? At 8:30.

SKILL OBJECTIVES: Third-person singular; simple present tense; asking questions. Have students read and discuss the doctor's routine. Do the first five items with the class, asking for volunteers to phrase questions 2 through 5. Then assign the page for independent written work. When students have completed the page, have them compare their questions.

32

Things People Do

Language Objective
Write and pronounce third-person singular present tense verbs correctly.

To change most verbs to the third-person singular, just add -s. If the verb ends in s, x, ch, or sh, add -es. The -es ending stands for the sound iz. When -s follows the letters ce, ge, or se, it is also pronounced iz.

I	like	You	ask	We	dance	They	push
He She It	} likes	The boy The girl The question	} asks	My friend Your friend The bear	} dances	This man That woman A snowplow	} pushes

A Complete the sentence by writing the correct form of the underlined verb. The first one is done for you.

1. Those children <u>like</u> cats. This child _____likes_____ dogs.

2. John and Mary <u>walk</u> to school together. Tomás _____ to school alone.

3. My brothers and I <u>watch</u> TV every night. Michelle _____ TV only on Thursdays.

4. My mother and father <u>drive</u> very carefully. My sister _____ too fast.

5. The eighth graders <u>want</u> to win the race. Nobody _____ to lose.

6. The Smoots <u>wash</u> their clothes on Sunday. Mrs. Perez _____ on Friday.

7. Good friends <u>call</u> each other often. My friend Molly _____ me every day.

8. I <u>change</u> my clothes when I get home from school. Erica _____ her clothes, too.

B Read the paragraph below. Write the missing words on the line. Use the verbs in the Data Bank. Add -s or -es to each verb. The first one is done for you.

Ramon Medina _____loves_____ to exercise. He is a physical fitness "nut." Every morning he _____ forty laps in the school swimming pool. In the afternoon he _____ basketball with his friends. Three times a week he _____ five miles. On Saturday mornings he _____ weights and _____ rope. On Saturday afternoons he _____ on boxing gloves and _____ with some of the guys at the gym. Sunday is Ramon's day for bicycling. He _____ his bike for miles until he _____ a nice spot for a picnic. On Sunday nights, Ramon _____ home. He _____ sports on television!

DATA BANK					
box	find	jump	lift	~~love~~	play
put	ride	run	stay	swim	watch

SKILL OBJECTIVE: Constructing third-person singular present tense: -s, -es, Read the example box aloud. Have students note how the spelling of each verb changes in the third-person singular. Have them note the sound represented by each final -s or -es. Go over the rules together. Write on the board: *I use, I fix, I want, I brush, I bake.* Have volunteers change these to third-person singular. Ask each student to use one of the verbs in a sentence. Do Part A orally before assigning the page as independent written work.

How They Live: Two Stories

Language Objective
Complete sentences with the correct form of the present tense.

Read the two stories below. Complete the sentences with words from the Data Bank. Watch for singular and plural subjects. Add -s or -es to the verbs in the Data Bank when needed. The first word has been filled in for you.

The Martin Family

René and Henriette Martin _____live_____ in Miami. René _____ in a hospital. Henriette _____ a dress shop. She _____ a lot of time in the store. The Martins _____ two children, Guy and Therese. Both children _____ the Traymore Vocational School. Guy _____ to be a plumber when he _____ school. Therese _____ on becoming an electrician. Mr. and Mrs. Martin _____ sure that their children _____ hard in school. They want their daughter and son to be successful.

DATA BANK A

attend	finish	have	hope	~~live~~	make	own	plan	spend	study	work

Isabel Valiente

Isabel Valiente is a professional photographer. She _____ all around the world. She _____ pictures of politicians and movie stars. Isabel _____ the celebrities to look natural. She _____ her camera quickly. She _____ her subjects yawning and laughing, looking thoughtful or surprised. Most famous people _____ publicity; they _____ having their pictures taken. However, some celebrities _____ to avoid Isabel's camera. They _____ to stay out of the public eye as much as possible. Isabel _____ her pictures to newspapers and magazines. Newspapers and magazines _____ lots of money for photographs of famous people, especially the ones who are "camera shy."

DATA BANK B

catch	enjoy	like	pay	prefer	sell	take	travel	try	use	want

SKILL OBJECTIVES: Constructing the present tense; choosing the correct form. Review the rules presented on page 33. If appropriate, provide additional oral practice with the skill. Read and complete the first few sentences of "The Martin Family" as a class, then assign the page for independent written work. Correct the page orally, asking volunteers to read the completed sentences aloud.

Writing About a Job

Read the story.

Language Objectives
Answer questions about a reading. Write a paragraph using third-person singular present tense verbs correctly.

During the spring and summer Mark and Oliva coach a baseball team. The players on the team they coach are all kids from the Jackie Robinson Elementary School. Mark and Oliva have a big job. They set up times for practices and games.

They pick a name for the team with the players. They decide that the name the Robinson Ribbies is great! Then Mark and Oliva order the uniforms for the players. After every game, Mark and Oliva take the team out for ice cream.

A **What is the main idea of this story? Circle your answer.**

a. A baseball team must have uniforms.

b. The players on the team are wonderful players.

c. Mark and Oliva set up games with other teams.

d. Mark and Oliva are baseball coaches during the spring and summer.

B **When the first-person singular form of a verb ends in a consonant followed by -y, change the -y to -ies to make the third-person singular. When the first-person singular form of the verb ends in a vowel followed by -y, just add -s to make the third-person singular. In both cases you pronounce (say) the word just as you pronounce the first-person form but with a z sound at the end of it.**

	He				He	
I try	She }	tries		I stay	She }	stays
	It				It	

Now rewrite the story to be about Ted, who is also a coach during the spring and summer. He coaches a team just like Mark and Oliva's team. Use the rule above. The first sentence is done for you.

During the spring and summer, Ted coaches a baseball team.

_____

_____

_____

_____

SKILL OBJECTIVES: Third-person singular present tense: -s, -es, -ies; identifying main idea. Read the paragraph aloud. Explain new words. Allow students to reread silently, then answer Part A. Discuss why choice *d* is the best answer. *Part B:* Review the verb rule with the students. Write on the board: *sway, pay, worry, enjoy, dry.* Ask volunteers to write the third-person singular of each verb. Ask others to use the verbs in oral sentences. You may wish to do the exercise as an oral activity before assigning as independent written work.

Whose Is It?

Language Objectives
Answer questions using possessive nouns. Complete sentences using possessive adjectives.

A Use the chart above to answer these questions. Answer in complete sentences. The first ones are done for you.

1. Whose umbrella is it?   It's Amy's umbrella.

2. Whose golf clubs are they?   They're Amy's golf clubs.

3. Whose cat is it?   _____

4. Whose shoes are they?   _____

5. Whose pen is it?   _____

6. Whose books are they?   _____

7. Whose car is it?   _____

8. Whose CDs are they?   _____

B Read each sentence. Then write the right word in the blank: *his*, *my*, our, *her*, or *their*.

1. She washes ____her____ hair every day.

2. Fred wants to borrow _____ father's car.

3. Roberto and I cook _____ dinner together every night.

4. Do you want to do _____ homework now?

5. My sister is looking for _____ keys.

6. The Rodriguez family is painting _____ house.

7. I seldom drive _____ car.

8. Johann and Erik are doing _____ laundry at the laundromat.

9. Lily and I are watching _____ favorite TV program.

SKILL OBJECTIVE: Using possessive nouns and adjectives. *Part A:* Borrow a student's book and ask, "Whose book is this?" Write the answer on the board: It's (Kim's) book. Call attention to the chart and the sample answers. Note the two uses of the apostrophe and have students explain their function. Do all or some of the items orally before assigning as written work. *Part B:* Review possessive adjectives. Have students rephrase item 1 using different pronouns and matching possessives. ("He washes his hair every day," etc.) You may wish to cover this Part orally before assigning it as independent written work.

The 911 Operator

Read the story.

Sara Lewis is a 911 operator. She answers the phone when people call 911. People call 911 when there is an emergency. This could be a fire, a traffic accident, or a medical emergency. People who do Sara's job have to work hard and very carefully, because sometimes other people's lives depend on their help.

Processing 911 calls is more complicated than you might think. When you call the number, the operator asks your name, telephone number, and address. The operator listens to your problem. Then she reads the information you gave back to you. Next, the operator calls the emergency worker who can help you.

If you are reporting a crime, such as a burglary, the operator will call the police department. If you report a fire, the operator will call the nearest fire department. If you report a medical emergency, the operator will call an ambulance service. Depending on the emergency, the police, a team of firefighters, or an emergency medical team will then report to the scene.

Now read the sentences below. Write a *T* if the sentence is true. Write an *F* if the sentence is false. Write a *?* if the story doesn't give you enough information to tell whether the sentence is true or false. The first two are done for you.

1. The 911 operator calls the fire department to report a burglary.   _F_

2. A 911 operator helps you in emergency situations.   _T_

3. You should call 911 if you lose your glasses.   _____

4. All 911 operators are paid very well.   _____

5. Lives can depend on 911 operators.   _____

6. A 911 operator writes down your name and telephone number.   _____

7. The 911 operator will check with you to make sure the information is correct.   _____

8. The police department is contacted if you report a fire.   _____

9. It's a fact that 911 operators are nice people.   _____

10. The operator contacts the hospital if you report a medical emergency.   _____

SKILL OBJECTIVES: Learning about 911; reading for details. Read the introductory paragraphs aloud, then have the class reread them silently. Let students discuss what they would do in the event of an emergency. Ask, "What information does the 911 operator need to help you?" Review the concept of the true/false/? type of exercise and discuss why the first two items are marked as they are. Then have students complete the page independently.

Do, Does, Don't, Doesn't

A Use *do* and *does* to ask questions in the present tense. See the box below.

| Do | { I you we they | have the right change? | Does | { he she it | work here? |

Complete each sentence with *do* or *does*.

1. _____ you always have toast and coffee for breakfast?

2. _____ Ramon swim forty laps in the pool every day?

3. _____ David travel to many different countries on his job?

4. _____ nurses take care of patients in hospitals?

5. _____ you plan to become an electrician?

6. _____ your assistant always type so quickly?

7. _____ it snow in Hawaii?

8. _____ the Costellos always take their vacation in Miami?

B Now look at this box.

| I We You They } | don't have the time. | He She It } | doesn't belong here. |

Complete each sentence with *don't* or *doesn't*.

1. In an emergency, you _____ have to fill out forms.

2. I _____ know my account number.

3. The bank _____ pay a lot of interest on a regular savings account.

4. Many students _____ read newspapers at home.

5. We _____ eat turkey on Thanksgiving at our house.

6. Your last name _____ belong in this space.

7. We _____ like pizza very much.

8. Shaaren and Rajiv _____ like to clean the house.

SKILL OBJECTIVE: Simple present tense with *do/does.* *Part A:* Explain/review the uses of *do* and *does* in the box at the top. Do the first two items together before assigning Part A for independent written work. *Part B:* Follow the same procedure as that for Part A.

38

Families

Here are the names of eight families:

Language Objective
Describe people with adjectives based on context clues about their behaviors.

The Clean Family	The Smart Family	The Happy Family	The Noisy Family
The Busy Family	The Quiet Family	The Tired Family	The Healthy Family

Read each of the following paragraphs. Write the name of the family it is describing. The first one is done for you.

1. We always talk very loud. Everyone talks at the same time. We have three dogs that always bark loudly. The TV is always on. We have parties every Saturday night.

   The Noisy Family

2. Everyone in our family is a college graduate. We read the encyclopedia for fun. Grandpa knows the meaning of every word in the Oxford English Dictionary.

   _____

3. We eat lots of fresh fruit and vegetables. We get lots of exercise. Everyone in this house gets a good night's sleep. We take our vitamins every day, too.

   _____

4. We sweep, we vacuum, we dust. There isn't any dirt in our house. Some of the people in this family take three showers a day. Even our cat gets a bath once a week.

   _____

5. Everyone in our family is a worker. We all have two jobs, or we go to work and to school. We don't have time to watch TV or read a book. We all have things to do, places to go, and people to see.

   _____

6. We never speak loudly. Everyone in our family whispers. We walk on tiptoe. Our dog, Silence, never barks.

   _____

7. Everyone in this family yawns all the time. We don't do too much. Father sometimes gets sleepy when he drives the car, so you have to be careful when you're riding with him. Uncle Albert can never get up on time.

   _____

8. We take long rides in the country together. We love to play and joke with each other. Sometimes at night the whole family gets together to talk. All our friends say that they love to come to visit us.

   _____

SKILL OBJECTIVES: Identifying topics; understanding characters' feelings. Read the names of the eight families aloud. Explain any unfamiliar adjectives. Ask a group of three students to come to the front of the class. Whisper the name of one of these families for the group to pantomime. The rest of the class must guess which family is being portrayed. Repeat this activity several times. Then assign the page for independent written work.

A Future Job

Do you have a job now? Are you looking for a job? Do you know what kind of job you want? Finding a job is not always easy, but some jobs are easier to find than others. The chart below shows about how many new workers are needed in the near future in various jobs in the United States and the average annual salaries for those jobs.

A Look at the chart and use it to complete the sentences under it. Use your dictionary if you are not sure of some of the vocabulary.

Jobs with the Most Openings (2000–2010)

Jobs	Number of Job Openings	Average Annual Salary (2003)
Registered nurse	1,004,000	$51,230
Vocational nurse	322,000	$33,210
Elementary school teacher	551,000	$44,350
Secondary school teacher	492,000	$46,790
Computer software engineer (systems software)	306,000	$78,400
Computer software engineer (applications)	406,000	$75,750
Computer systems analyst	296,000	$66,180
Computer support specialist	512,000	$42,640
Automotive service technician and mechanic	349,000	$33,320
Cook (restaurant)	335,000	$20,020
Accountant and auditor	326,000	$55,430
Carpenter	302,000	$36,920
Police officer	269,000	$44,960

Source: U.S. Bureau of Labor Statistics

1. There are about _____ openings for registered nurses.

2. There are about _____ openings for computer software engineers (systems software) and _____ openings for computer software engineers (applications).

3. The total number of openings for cooks and carpenters is about _____.

4. The total number of openings for accountants and auditors is _____.

5. The education industry needs about _____ teachers altogether.

6. Computer systems analysts earn $_____ more than computer support specialists.

7. Vocational nurses earn $_____ less than registered nurses.

SKILL OBJECTIVES: Learning about job openings and salaries in the United States; adding to find a total; subtracting to find the difference. Discuss jobs students have had and/or would like to have. Then discuss the chart, what it shows and what it does not show (it doesn't show how many people are employed in the occupations, for example, but only how many new openings are estimated up to 2010). Explain new vocabulary. Have students read the numbers aloud. *Part A:* Do the first two items orally with the group, then assign for independent written work.

What Are They Doing?

Language Objective
Tell what people are doing through the use of context clues.

Read the information and choose an answer from the Data Bank to tell what each person is doing. The first one is done for you.

1. Boris is standing at home plate. He is swinging a bat and hitting a ball.

   What is he doing?   _He's playing baseball._

2. Paul and Joanne are mixing flour, eggs, butter, and sugar. They are turning on the oven.

   What are they doing? _____

3. Marco is sitting at his desk. He is holding a pen and writing on some paper. There is an envelope on the desk, too.

   What is he doing? _____

4. David is at the laundromat. He is putting detergent in one of the machines. He is putting coins into the slots.

   What is he doing? _____

5. Maria and her friends are listening to music. They are moving their feet, swinging their arms, and shaking their hair.

   What are they doing? _____

6. Paula Jenkins is walking from house to house. She is carrying a bag of letters, magazines, and newspapers.

   What is she doing? _____

7. The Nguyens are going to many different stores. They are looking at tables, chairs, sofas, bookcases, and bureaus.

   What are they doing? _____

8. The students are sitting at their desks quietly. Some are writing and some are erasing and changing their answers.

   What are they doing? _____

9. Raisa is not eating any sugar or snacks. She is jogging every morning and riding her bicycle every afternoon.

   What is she doing? _____

10. Veronica is planning the menu. Jorge is renting the hall. Both of them are inviting the guests to the church and the reception.

    What are they doing? _____

DATA BANK

dancing	planning a wedding	buying furniture	making a cake
trying to lose weight	taking a test	delivering the mail	
~~playing baseball~~	writing a letter	washing his clothes	

SKILL OBJECTIVES: **Drawing conclusions; reviewing the present progressive tense; building vocabulary.** Do the first two or three items orally before assigning the page as independent written work. Remind students that the answers are all in the Data Bank.

Helping You Study:
Using the Dictionary (2)

On page 30 you learned what part of the dictionary to find your word in. But you also need to know what page the word is on. To help you, the dictionary has guide words at the top of each page. These guide words are the first and last words on the page.

1. Look at the illustration. What is the first word on the page?

   _____

2. What is the last word on the same page?

   _____

Look at the sets of guide words below. Under each set of guide words are six other words. Decide which of these six words belong on the page with that set of guide words. If the word belongs on the page, write *Yes*. If it does not belong on the page, write *No*.

Baby	Bottle
book	Yes
barn	_____
battle	_____
bill	_____
break	_____
best	_____

Light	Lucky
lollipop	_____
late	_____
lend	_____
lots	_____
luck	_____
like	_____

Sick	Stay
socks	_____
spend	_____
see	_____
stupid	_____
stand	_____
sell	_____

Quart	Quorum
quiet	_____
quick	_____
question	_____
quack	_____
quit	_____
quote	_____

Corn	Cruel
crust	_____
cruise	_____
cove	_____
cold	_____
crab	_____
cry	_____

Eclipse	Enamel
éclair	_____
educate	_____
error	_____
effect	_____
end	_____
entire	_____

SKILL OBJECTIVE: Using guide words. Read the explanatory paragraph aloud. Let the class answer the guide word questions together. If possible, have students open dictionaries and note the use of guide words. Read the directions to the exercise, and do the first set or two as a group activity. If a word does *not* belong on the page, ask students if they would find it on the pages *before* or *after*. Assign the rest of the exercise as independent written work. Correct the page together.

Dear Dot

Language Objectives
Answer questions about a reading. Give advice. Agree or disagree with advice.

Dear Dot

Dear Dot,
   My family is driving me crazy, I like to be the first person in the bathroom in the morning. I get up at 6:00 a.m., and I take my shower. Then I comb my hair, brush my teeth, put on my makeup, and give a little smile in the mirror—just to make sure I look okay. Before I finish, my father and mother are knocking at he door, and my brother and sister are yelling, "Hurry up!" Of course, this ruins the morning, and everyone is in a bad mood at breakfast. What can I do?

                                                          Maria

1. Who is driving Maria crazy? _____

2. When does Maria get up? _____

3. Why does Maria smile at the mirror? _____

_____

4. What do her brother and sister yell? _____

5. Why is everyone in a bad mood at breakfast? _____

_____

6. What does the word *yelling* in this letter mean? Circle the best answer.

   a. talking   **b.** playing   **c.** telling   **d.** screaming

7. What is your advice to Maria? Discuss with your classmates what she ought and ought not to do. Then play the part of Dot and write your answer to her.

   ___Dear Maria,_____

   _____

   _____

   _____

   _____

   _____

   _____

                                          _____

SKILL OBJECTIVES: Reading comprehension; understanding words through context; making judgments; writing a letter. Read the letter aloud or have a volunteer read it. Explain any unfamiliar words. Ask students to tell what "drives them crazy" or puts them in a bad mood. Have them reread the letter silently and answer questions 1–6. Correct these items. Then tell students that they are going to write Dot's answer to Maria. Have them discuss what their advice should be, then have them work independently to write their letters. Help them with letter format, if necessary.

43

Language Objective
Talk about future plans using
the <u>be going to</u> form.

When we make plans for the future, we use a form of the verb *to be*, plus *going to*, followed by the verb. See the examples in the box below.

PLANNING TO DO WHAT?		WHEN?
I *am going to* go to Hawaii.	We *are going to* have fun.	Next week
He *is going to* swim.	You *are going to* relax.	Tomorrow
She *is going to* play tennis.	They *are going to* stay at a hotel.	In three days
It *is going to* be sunny.		Next winter

A Amy, Hugo, Pam, and Lynn are making plans for their vacations. Use the travel ads above to answer these questions about their plans.

1. Where is Amy going to go?

_____

2. How is she going to travel?

_____

3. Where is she going to stay?

_____

4. How long is she going to be there?

_____

5. What is she going to do there?

_____

6. How much is her vacation going to cost?

_____

(Go on to the next page.)

SKILL OBJECTIVES: Future form: *be going to*; reading travel ads; asking/answering questions. Have students look at the vacation ads and the box reviewing the *be going to* structures. *Part A:* Call attention to Amy's plan to go to Hawaii, and ask the six questions. Have students answer orally in complete sentences, then write their sentences.

B

1. Where are Pam and Lynn going to go?

_____

2. How are they going to get there?

_____

3. Where are they going to stay?

_____

4. How long are they going to be there?

_____

5. What are they going to do there?

_____

6. How much is their vacation going to cost?

_____

C In your notebook, write questions and answers about Hugo's vacation. Use the questions in Parts A and B as guides.

D What about you? Imagine that you have just won $2,000. Now you can take your dream vacation! In your notebook, write answers to these questions about your dream vacation.

1. Where are you going to go?

2. How are you going to get there?

3. When are you going to go?

4. What are you going to do or see?

5. How long are you going to stay?

6. Are you going to go with your family?

7. Are you going to stay at a hotel?

8. How much is your vacation going to cost?

E Now write about your dream vacation in paragraph form. Think of a good beginning sentence and a good ending sentence.

_____

_____

_____

_____

_____

_____

_____

SKILL OBJECTIVES: Asking/answering questions; writing a paragraph. *Part B:* Follow the same procedure as for Part A on the facing page, but this time do only sentence 1 orally. *Part C:* Have students write both the questions and the answers for Hugo in their notebooks. Use the same six questions but with the pronoun *he*. *Part D:* Discuss these questions, then have students write their answer in their notebooks. *Part E:* Have them use their answers from Part D as a source for their paragraph-form description. Discuss the idea of having their first sentence be a topic sentence and their last sentence be a summary.

The Festival of Las Fallas

Language Objective
Answer questions about a reading.

Read the article.

Las Fallas is a festival that takes place every spring in Valencia, a city in Spain. The festival's name is pronounced *lahs FIE-yas*.

In preparation for the festival, people in each Valencia neighborhood build statues from papier-mâché—a material made with wet paper—and a special kind of paste. These statues are called *fallas*, and they give the festival its name. The Spanish word *fallas* means "bonfire." And that's what the statues are made for—a city-wide bonfire. Many of the statues are very funny. The statues make fun of famous people. Sometimes they make fun of people who live in Valencia. Some of the statues are twenty feet tall!

No one remembers exactly why the first *fallas* were made. But all year long the teams from each neighborhood meet and plan and raise money to make a statue that they will burn up. *Fallas* are expensive to make. Each neighborhood needs to raise several thousand dollars. The people who make each statue form a team, with a leader. The finished statues are judged in a competition.

Regardless of which statue wins the contest, the statues all require a lot of hard work. That is why what happens to them is so surprising. In the middle of the festival, the people of Valencia set fire to the statues. They stuff the statues with fireworks, light them, and watch the statues explode into flames. *Las Fallas* brings the people of Valencia together. Music plays, parades pass through the city, and there is excitement everywhere.

A **Now answer these questions. The first one is done for you.**

1. Where is Valencia?   <u>It is a city in Spain.</u>

2. What is Las Fallas? _____

3. When does Las Fallas take place? _____

4. What do people do to prepare for the festival? _____

5. What is papier-mâché? _____

6. What do the statues look like? _____

7. What happens to the statues? _____

8. Do you think the people of Valencia have firefighters on guard during Las Fallas? _____

B **What is the article mostly about? Circle the best answer.**

a. Valencia

b. fireworks

c. the festival of Las Fallas

d. papier-mâché

SKILL OBJECTIVES: Identifying main idea and details. Read the article aloud. Explain any unfamiliar vocabulary. Help students locate Spain, then the city of Valencia, on a map. Ask students to reread the article, then complete Parts A and B independently. Correct as a class. Make sure students understand why choice *c* is the best answer to Part B. Ask students if they would like to go to Valencia and take part in Las Fallas. Why or why not? Encourage lively discussion.

Choose the Right Word

Complete each sentence with one of the following words or pairs of words: _in, on, at, to, from, next to, before, after_. The first one is done for you.

1. Pedro is _____from_____ Cuba.

2. She always goes to the supermarket _____ Friday.

3. Bill went to the movies _____ nine o'clock.

4. Sue and Jan went for a walk _____ the park.

5. Mary is writing a letter _____ her mother.

6. Always wash your hands _____ you eat.

7. What time do you get up _____ the morning?

8. The Rodriguez family lives _____ the Mahood family.

9. We go _____ the movies every Saturday.

10. Vicente is waiting _____ the bus stop.

11. She is going to Puerto Rico _____ July.

12. November comes _____ October.

13. Harry works _____ the office _____ the first floor.

14. Bruno likes to sit _____ me at lunch.

15. The bank is _____ the corner of Dudley Street and Columbia Road.

16. It's raining _____ Miami today.

17. We get letters _____ Juan every week.

18. Chiara is talking _____ the teacher.

19. He is looking _____ the pictures in the museum.

20. October always comes _____ November.

21. Monday always comes _____ Sunday.

22. Where is he _____ ?

23. Please sit _____ the red chair.

24. What does Alex do _____ Monday?

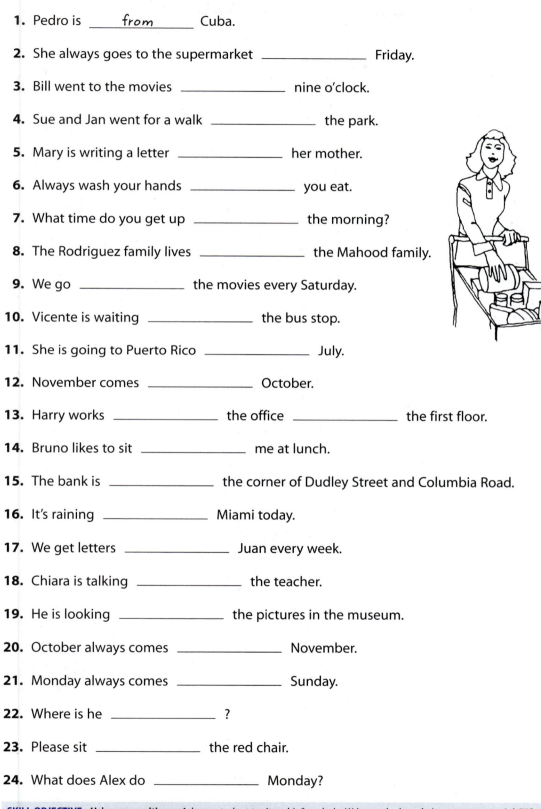

What Are They Going to Do?

Each of these people has a problem. What is he or she going to do? Write an answer for each problem.

1. Mr. Gonzales leaves his house. His car has a flat tire. He has to get to work soon. What is he going to do?

   _____

   _____

2. Laura comes home late from work. Her house is a mess. The beds aren't made, and there are dirty dishes in the sink. Friends are coming over to visit in thirty minutes. What is she going to do?

   _____

   _____

3. Paul has a problem. He doesn't have his front door key. His parents are out visiting friends. His brother has a key, but Paul can't find him. What is Paul going to do?

   _____

   _____

4. The Wongs live in a very small five-room apartment. There are eight people in the Wong family. They need more space to live in. They don't like their apartment anymore. What are they going to do?

   _____

   _____

5. Rosa is sick. This is the third day that she has to stay in bed. She is taking aspirin. She is drinking lots of liquid, but she isn't feeling any better. What is she going to do?

   _____

   _____

(Go on to the next page.)

SKILL OBJECTIVES: **Making predictions; creative problem solving.** This page and the following present a number of creative problem-solving situations. Both pages can be effectively used in oral group activity. Read each situation aloud. Explain unfamiliar words. Encourage students to suggest as many different solutions as possible. As an incentive, keep a tally of the number of solutions offered for each situation. After all ten items have been discussed, assign the pages for independent written work. Students should choose one solution to write after each problem.

48

6. Deborah walks into her apartment. It is freezing. She turns on the heat, but nothing happens. Deborah goes downstairs to the basement. Something is wrong with the furnace. There is no heat in the house. What is she going to do?

_____

_____

7. Vinh is at a school dance. He sees a beautiful girl across the room. She sees him. They smile at each other. The band begins to play a slow song. Vinh walks over to her. What is he going to do?

_____

_____

8. Margarita gets a headache when she reads for a long time. She can't see objects that are far away. Sometimes her eyes hurt her. What is she going to do?

_____

_____

9. Mr. Lee is the boss at Bigcorp Computers. Jack, one of his employees, is almost always late. Many other days Jack calls in sick or leaves work early. Today he is two hours late. What is Mr. Lee going to do?

_____

_____

10. The baby is crying. The dog is barking. Cars and trucks are passing by and making noises. Mr. Mleczko is watching the news on TV. He can't hear a thing. What is he going to do?

_____

_____

SKILL OBJECTIVES: Making predictions; creative problem solving. See annotation on page 48.

49

In, On, Under

Where can you find each of the sets of things on the left? The column on the right has the answers. Write the letter of the right answer in the blank for each set of things. Use each answer only once. The first one is done for you.

1. stars, sun, moon   _q_   **a.** in a living room
2. principal, teachers, students   _____   **b.** on a field
3. candies, frosting, icing   _____   **c.** in the Pacific Ocean
4. Empire State Building, Broadway, Statue of Liberty   _____   **d.** on a boat
5. milk, butter, cheese   _____   **e.** on a wall
6. cows, chickens, barn   _____   **f.** on a face
7. sofa, television, armchair   _____   **g.** on trees
8. dust, shoes, slippers   _____   **h.** under the ground
9. Spain, France, Britain   _____   **i.** in a restaurant
10. pictures, posters, light-switch   _____   **j.** in a school
11. sailors, cabins, deck   _____   **k.** under the sea
12. shower, sink, toilet   _____   **l.** in the refrigerator
13. lions, tigers, elephants   _____   **m.** in a garden
14. traffic, subway, buildings   _____   **n.** on a farm
15. nose, eyes, mouth   _____   **o.** in a closet
16. shells, shipwrecks, cables   _____   **p.** on a cake
17. coats, hats, dresses   _____   **q.** in the sky
18. flowers, tomatoes, corn   _____   **r.** in a city
19. pots, pans, kettle   _____   **s.** in a zoo
20. bones, blood, heart   _____   **t.** on a stove
21. players, goal posts, soccer ball   _____   **u.** under the skin
22. apples, bananas, oranges   _____   **v.** in jars
23. subway, pipes, wires   _____   **w.** in the bathroom
24. Hawaii, Japan, the Philippines   _____   **x.** in Europe
25. pickles, peanut butter, jelly   _____   **y.** under the bed
26. tables, waiters, menus   _____   **z.** in New York City

Menu

SKILL OBJECTIVES: Using prepositional phrases; classifying. Do several times as an oral group exercise, then assign the page as independent written work. To correct, have students cover the right hand column and try to recall the prepositional phrase as you ask, "Where can you find …?"

50

A Good Friend

Read the story.

Language Objective
Answer questions about a reading. Rearrange statements to show a correct sequence.

Clara Hart is a nurse at Wedgewood Elementary School. She arrives at work at 8:00 a.m. She prepares for the day ahead. She straightens up her office and makes sure she has enough supplies.

At 10:30, Bobby comes into the office with a cut thumb. Clara washes the cut and puts a bandage on it. At 11:30, Sally comes into the office. She has her hand on her head and is crying. When Clara asks Sally what is wrong, Sally says her head hurts and she feels hot. Clara takes Sally's temperature and finds that she has a fever. She calls Sally's mother to come and take Sally home. Clara stays with Sally until her mother arrives.

At 1:00, Tim comes in to see Clara. Tim is in the first grade. He has asthma and sometimes needs to use his inhaler. Clara keeps Tim's inhaler in her closet. She gives Tim the inhaler and he squirts the medicine into his mouth. Tim sits for a few minutes until he can breathe better, then he goes back to class.

So far there have been no emergencies for Clara, but the day isn't over yet.

A Now answer these questions. Use short answers.

1. Where does Clara Hart work?

_____

2. When does she get to work?

_____

3. When does Bobby come into her office?

_____

4. Who will pick Sally up from school?

_____

5. Why does Tim need Clara's help?

_____

B Which of the following statements is most likely true about Clara? Circle your answer.

a. She likes taking care of people.   **c.** She likes hiking.

b. She teaches biology.   **d.** She is a school counselor.

C Put numbers on the line before each statement to show the correct order. The number 1 is done for you.

_____ Clara takes Sally's temperature.   _____ Sally says her head hurts.

_____ Bobby comes into the office.   _____ Clara calls Sally's mother.

_____ Sally comes into the office.   _____ Clara puts a bandage on Bobby's thumb.

___1___ Clara arrives at the school.   _____ Clara gives Tim his asthma medicine.

_____ Tim comes to see Clara.

SKILL OBJECTIVES: Identifying main idea and details; making inferences; sequencing. Read the story aloud. Explain any unfamiliar words. Have students reread the story before answering the comprehension questions independently. Correct and discuss the answers as a class.

Helping You Study: Alphabetical Order (3)

A When you alphabetize people's names, you put the last name first, then the first name and middle name or initial (if it is given). Rewrite these famous names this way. Then write them in alphabetical order. The first line in each column is done for you.

	Rewrite	**Alphabetize**
Thomas Edison	_Edison, Thomas_	_Alcott, Louisa May_
Christopher Columbus	_____	_____
Harriet Beecher Stowe	_____	_____
George Washington	_____	_____
Louisa May Alcott	_____	_____
Susan B. Anthony	_____	_____
Martin Luther King, Jr.	_____	_____
Alexander Graham Bell	_____	_____
Neil Armstrong	_____	_____
Nancy Lopez	_____	_____

B After your teacher corrects your work, or you are sure that you are correct, do these names the same way.

Noah Webster	_____	_____
Harriet Tubman	_____	_____
Stephen Austin	_____	_____
Henry Aaron	_____	_____
Annie Oakley	_____	_____
Jonas Salk	_____	_____
Eleanor Roosevelt	_____	_____
Helen Keller	_____	_____
Amelia Earhart	_____	_____
Jesse James	_____	_____

SKILL OBJECTIVE: Listing people alphabetically by last names. Write several student names on the board. Ask the class how you would find a certain student's number in the phone book. Establish that last names are listed alphabetically. As a group, rewrite the students' names, last name first, then alphabetize the list. Assign the page as independent written work. *Extension Activities:* 1) How many of the listed names can the class identify? 2) Help students draw up an alphabetized class directory with addresses and phone numbers.

Dear Dot

Language Objectives
Answer questions about a reading. Give advice. Agree or disagree with advice.

Dear Dot,

My family moves around a lot. Every year I go to a different school. Sometimes the work is boring, because I know all the subjects already. Other times, the work is all new to me, and I don't understand it. This year I like my school a lot. The work is interesting, and I have many friends. Now my mother says we are going to leave this town and go to another state. I don't want to leave. What can I do?

Happy Where I Am

1. Why does Happy go to so many different schools? _____

_____

2. Why is school sometimes boring for Happy? _____

_____

3. Why is it too difficult other times? _____

_____

4. What did Happy's mother tell him? _____

_____

5. How does Happy feel about the news? _____

6. What does the word *boring* in this letter mean? Circle the best answer.

   a. difficult   **b.** lively   **c.** fascinating   **d.** uninteresting

7. Talk with your classmates about what Happy should do. Then write your answer to him.

   Dear Happy Where I Am, _____

   _____

   _____

   _____

   _____

   _____

SKILL OBJECTIVES: **Reading comprehension; understanding words through context; making judgments; writing a letter.** Read the letter aloud or have a volunteer read it. Explain any unfamiliar words. Ask students to reread the letter silently and answer questions 1–6. Correct these items. Then have the students discuss what their advice to Happy would be; finally have them write Dot's answer, incorporating this advice.

A riddle is a question with a silly or unexpected answer. Here are some riddles. The answers are in the column at the right. Write the letter of the correct answer in the blank in front of the riddle. The first one is done for you.

1. Why do birds fly south for the winter? ___g___

2. What never asks questions but gets lots of answers? _____

3. Ten people are walking under one small umbrella. They aren't getting wet. Why not? _____

4. How can you spell "mousetrap" in three letters? _____

5. How can you keep a fish from smelling? _____

6. What has a neck but no head? _____

7. What kind of dress do you have but don't wear? _____

8. What comes once in a minute, once in a month, but never in a thousand years? _____

9. What do you take off last before you go to bed? _____

10. What is everyone in the world doing at the same time? _____

11. What has one eye open but cannot see? _____

12. What has four legs, a back, and two arms but cannot move? _____

13. If a woman is born in Spain, grows up in Japan, and dies in the U.S., what is she? _____

14. What always smiles and frowns when you do, but parts its hair on the other side? _____

15. What is the longest word in the English language? _____

a. The letter *m*

b. A chair

c. Your mirror image

d. Your address

e. Your feet on the floor

f. Cut off its nose.

g. It's too far to walk.

h. The doorbell

i. A bottle

j. Getting older

k. Dead

l. A needle

m. Smiles (There's a mile between the two *s*'s.)

n. C-A-T

o. It isn't raining.

SKILL OBJECTIVE: Understanding riddles. Solve the first few riddles as a group, then let students complete the page independently or in pairs. *Extension Activities:* 1) Help students locate the joke and riddle books, if any, in their school library, or find some on the Internet. 2) Plan a time for students to tell new jokes and riddles to their classmates. 3) Establish a corner of the bulletin board where students can post favorite comic strips from the newspaper or jokes and riddles they have read or heard.

The Simple Past Tense

Language Objective
Talk about picture prompts using the simple past tense.

The simple past tense is used to talk about activities or situations that began or ended in the past, for example, "Julio stayed home yesterday," "It rained all night long." Most simple past tense verbs are formed by adding -ed to the verb.

Forms of the Simple Past

Statement: I (you / he / she / it / we / they) worked yesterday.

Question: Did I (you / he / she / it / we / they) work yesterday?

Write a sentence under each picture. Use the correct past tense verb from the Data Bank. (One of the words is used twice.) The first one is done for you.

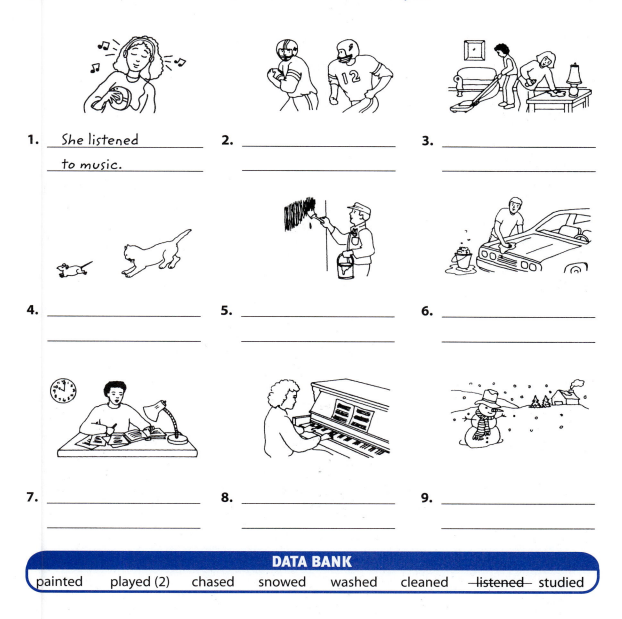

1. She listened to music.

2. _____

3. _____

4. _____

5. _____

6. _____

7. _____

8. _____

9. _____

DATA BANK

painted   played (2)   chased   snowed   washed   cleaned   ~~listened~~   studied

---

SKILL OBJECTIVES: **Forming past tense of regular verbs; writing sentences.** Write on the board, *What did you do yesterday?* Ask individual students such questions as, "Did you watch TV? What programs did you see?" "Did you listen to music?" etc. Read the explanation of the simple past tense and the forms of the simple past. Have the class look at item 1. Explain that in each item, *-ed* is added to the verb to form the simple past. Call attention to the Data Bank, then do the nine items orally before having students write the sentences.

What Did They Do?

Language Objective
Spell and pronounce the past tense of verbs correctly.

To change most verbs to the past tense, add *-ed*. If the verb ends in *e*, just add *-d*.

walk ➜ Yesterday, they walked.   *bike* ➜ Last Monday, they biked.

The *-ed* ending can stand for three different sounds, *d*, *t*, and *id*. Say the sentence for each picture. Then write the correct verb from the Data Bank on the line. The first one is done for you.

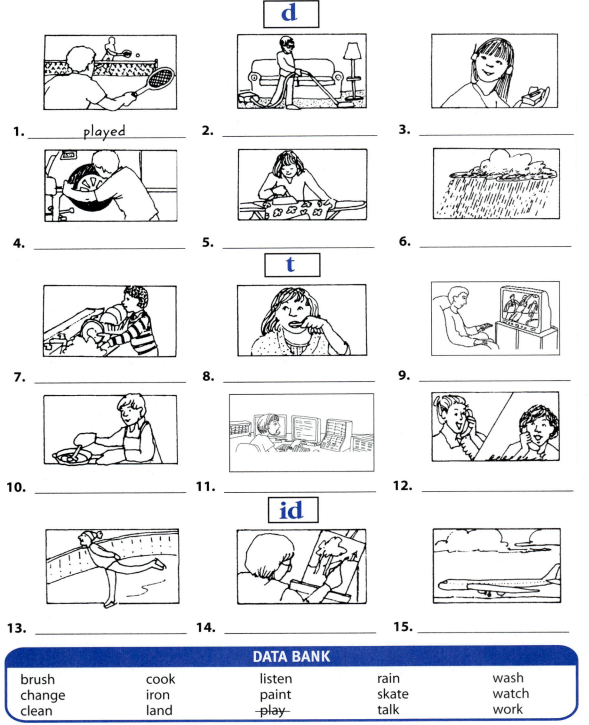

d

1. _____played_____   2. _____   3. _____

4. _____   5. _____   6. _____

t

7. _____   8. _____   9. _____

10. _____   11. _____   12. _____

id

13. _____   14. _____   15. _____

DATA BANK

brush	cook	listen	rain	wash
change	iron	paint	skate	watch
clean	land	~~play~~	talk	work

SKILL OBJECTIVES: Forming simple past tense; pronunciation of final -ed. Review the rule and examples. Work with the first block of pictures: *-ed* as *d*. Say a sentence for each picture: "Yesterday she ironed her blouse." Have students identify the picture and repeat the sentence. Repeat with the other two blocks of pictures. Next, have each student question the person on his/her left. *Student A*: "Number (9) What did he do yesterday?" *Student B*: "He watched TV. (to Student C) Number (6). What did it do yesterday?" Correct students' pronunciation. Assign the page for independent written work.

How Does It Sound?

Your teacher will read you each of the verbs in the box. Listen to the ending sound of each verb. Some of the verbs end with a *d* sound. Some of them end with a *t* sound. Some of them end with the sound of *id*. As your teacher reads each of the verbs, decide which sound it ends with, and write it in the correct column under the box. The first three are done for you.

Language Objective

Distinguish between the different sounds of the simple past tense.

~~ironed~~	closed	cleaned
~~painted~~	wanted	washed
~~polished~~	watched	baked
played	delivered	hated
kissed	brushed	traveled
typed	rented	planted
corrected	waited	parked
changed	arrived	called
worked	tasted	landed
fixed	opened	dated

d	t	id
1. _ironed_	1. _polished_	1. _painted_
2. _____	2. _____	2. _____
3. _____	3. _____	3. _____
4. _____	4. _____	4. _____
5. _____	5. _____	5. _____
6. _____	6. _____	6. _____
7. _____	7. _____	7. _____
8. _____	8. _____	8. _____
9. _____	9. _____	9. _____
10. _____	10. _____	10. _____

SKILL OBJECTIVES: Simple past tense; distinguishing among the three sounds of -ed. Pronounce each verb. Have students repeat, paying particular attention to the final *-ed* sound. As a group, decide in which column the word belongs. Allow time for writing. *Extension Activity:* Have students use the past tense verbs in original oral sentences.

Adding -ed

There are some important spelling rules to know when you add -ed to form the past tense. (These rules work for most words, but there are exceptions.)

Rule 1:	For most words, add -ed with no change.
	Examples: paint → painted rent → rented
Rule 2:	For words that end in e, drop the e and add -ed.
	Examples: type → typed close → closed
Rule 3:	For words that end in a consonant + y, change y to i and add -ed.
	Examples: hurry → hurried marry → married
Rule 4:	For one-syllable words that end in consonant + vowel + consonant (except w, x, y), double the final letter and add -ed.
	Examples: rob → robbed bag → bagged

A Now use these rules to add -ed to the following words.

1. serve _____
2. ask _____
3. try _____
4. love _____
5. arrest _____
6. stay _____
7. rain _____
8. lift _____
9. study _____
10. cook _____
11. chase _____
12. like _____
13. show _____
14. push _____
15. move _____

16. design _____
17. direct _____
18. announce _____
19. stop _____
20. live _____
21. match _____
22. clean _____
23. bark _____
24. help _____
25. carry _____
26. dance _____
27. learn _____
28. smile _____
29. repair _____
30. snow _____

31. cash _____
32. install _____
33. talk _____
34. practice _____
35. play _____
36. empty _____
37. end _____
38. listen _____
39. yawn _____
40. hope _____
41. pass _____
42. mix _____
43. use _____
44. cry _____
45. visit _____

B In your notebook, write sentences for fifteen of the past tense (-ed) words you wrote above. Use words such as *yesterday*, *last week*, and *ago* to show the past tense.

SKILL OBJECTIVE: Forming simple past tense, observing spelling changes. Go over the four rules at the top of the page; elicit additional examples. *Part A:* Complete the first several items as a class, having volunteers write the correct past tense form on the board. Then assign Part A as independent written work. *Part B:* Ask volunteers to make up sample sentences using the first three or four verbs and including cue words (*yesterday, etc.*) to emphasize that the sentence refers to something in the past. Then have students write their fifteen (or more if they wish) sentences. You may wish to have each student read his/her favorite sentence aloud.

A Time Line

A time line gives information in chronological order, that is, the order in which it happened. It shows what things happened at different times. Read this time line from left to right. It shows some things that happened to one person from 1995 through 2004.

Language Objectives
Answer past tense questions using specific dates. Create a personal time line.

Ten Years of Nancy Riley's Life

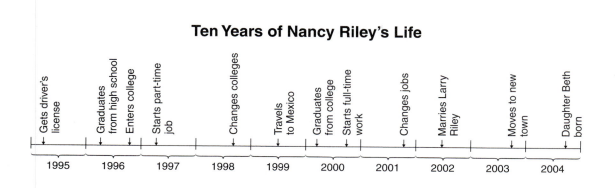

A Use the time line to answer these questions. Write the year.

1. When did Nancy travel to Mexico?   In the year _____

2. When did Nancy get a driver's license?   In the year _____

3. When did Nancy start a full-time job?   In the year _____

4. When did Nancy enter college?   In the year _____

5. When did Nancy marry Larry Riley?   In the year _____

6. When did Nancy graduate from college?   In the year _____

7. When did Nancy change colleges?   In the year _____

8. When did Nancy graduate from high school?   In the year _____

9. When did Nancy start her part-time job?   In the year _____

10. When did Nancy move to a new town?   In the year _____

B What about you? Fill in this time line for yourself. Put in important events in your own life. List the years below the line.

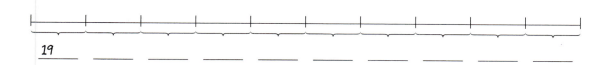

SKILL OBJECTIVES: Interpreting and charting a time line. Examine the time line with the students. Read the dates and events aloud together. Explain any unfamiliar words. Answer the first few questions as a group activity. Make sure students know how to use the chart to locate information, then assign the page for independent written work. Provide help with Part B as needed. *Extension Activity:* Have students form pairs and ask their partner questions about his/her time line: "Did you . . . (move to Virginia) in 1995?"

It's a Record!

A Before you read the article, look at the Vocabulary Preview. Be sure
that you know the meaning of each word. Use the dictionary. Some words have more
than one meaning. The way the word is used in the article will help you decide the
meaning you want. Write down the meanings of the words you are not sure of.

Vocabulary Preview			
unusual	_____	locations	_____
incredible	_____	athlete	_____
balanced	_____	competition	_____
crates	_____	traffic	_____
muscles	_____	limousine	_____

B Now read the article. Use the dictionary if there are other words that you are not sure
of. Notice that the words from the Vocabulary Preview are underlined.

The entries in the *Guinness Book of World Records* tell about <u>unusual</u> places, people, or things. The people who are in the book have set records by doing <u>incredible</u> things—something faster, better, or longer than anyone else. The places, on the other hand, have unusual characteristics—the hottest place in North America or the highest point on earth are two examples.

What things do people do that get their names and what they did in the book? Kirsten O'Brien holds the record for the most socks worn on one foot. She put forty-one socks on one of her feet during a talk show in London in 2003.

John Evans, also of the United Kingdom, <u>balanced</u> ninety-six milk <u>crates</u> on his head in 2001, setting another

record. He has been building his neck <u>muscles</u> since he was 18 years old.

The Olympic Games, held every four years at different <u>locations</u> around the world, lead to many records. The youngest ever Olympic champion <u>athlete</u> was the United States' Marjorie Gestring, 13 years old. She led in the springboard diving <u>competition</u>.

There are other kinds of records as well, set not by people but by events. For instance, the longest <u>traffic</u> jam in history happened in France, near the city of Lyon, in 1980. It was 109 miles long.

The longest car in the world is a <u>limousine</u> 100 feet long. It was designed by Jay Ohrberg of California. It contains a waterbed and a swimming pool (with a diving board).

(Go on to the next page.)

SKILL OBJECTIVES: Reading comprehension: building vocabulary; using simple past tense. Allow time for students to look up
vocabulary words in the dictionary and choose the appropriate definitions. Review the definitions together. If you wish, read the
article aloud before asking students to read it silently.

C **Use a word from the Vocabulary Preview to complete each of these sentences.**

1. Ilhan thought the museum was very _____ .

2. Suzy _____ the three books on her head.

3. I have never ridden in a _____ .

4. You should exercise to build up your _____ .

5. Everybody thought Deke was an excellent _____ .

D **Now answer these questions. Use complete sentences. The first one is done for you.**

1. How many socks did Kirsten O'Brien put on? *She put forty-one socks on one foot.*

2. Where did Kirsten do this? _____

3. What did John Evans do to get in the Guinness book? _____

4. How long had he been building his neck muscles? _____

5. What was special about Marjorie Gestring? _____

_____

6. What competition did Marjorie win? _____

7. Where did the longest traffic jam in history take place? _____

_____

8. How long was that traffic jam? _____

9. Who designed the longest car in the world? _____

10. What strange things did he add to it? _____

_____

SKILL OBJECTIVES: Reading comprehension: building vocabulary; using simple past tense. Students should complete the exercises independently. *Expansion Activities:* Help students locate collections of strange and unusual facts in the library. If your newspaper carries a column or fillers about unusual records, have students collect and share the clippings. Encourage students to report strange bits of knowledge to the class, then pose their facts in a "That's Incredible!" display.

61

Helping You Study: Using the Encyclopedia

Read the article.

You use the dictionary to look up the meaning of a word. If you want more information, you can look in an encyclopedia. Encyclopedias give information about people, places, things, events, and ideas.

The information in the encyclopedia, like the information in the dictionary, is in alphabetical order. Because encyclopedias contain more information about a subject than dictionaries do, most of them have several books or volumes. The letters on the outside of each volume tell you which words are in that volume. They usually are the first few letters of the first and last words in the volume.

Look at the encyclopedia below. Notice that there are thirty volumes. Each volume has a number on it, as well as the letters that tell what words are in it. Write the number of the volume in which you can look for information about each of the people on the list. Remember that people are always listed by their last name. The first one is done for you.

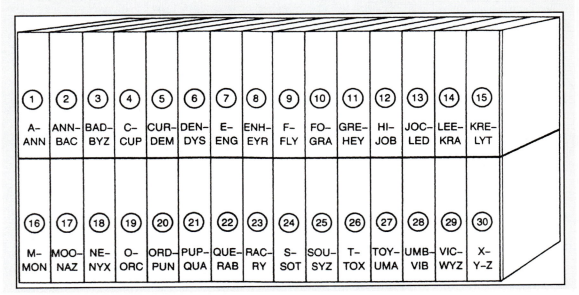

Write the number of the encyclopedia where you find:

Thomas Edison	7	Noah Webster	_____
Christopher Columbus	_____	Harriet Tubman	_____
Harriet Beecher Stowe	_____	Stephen Austin	_____
George Washington	_____	John Quincy Adams	_____
Louisa May Alcott	_____	Annie Oakley	_____
Susan B. Anthony	_____	Jonas Salk	_____
Alexander Graham Bell	_____	Eleanor Roosevelt	_____
Neil Armstrong	_____	Helen Keller	_____
Orville and Wilbur Wright	_____	Amelia Earhart	_____

When Did It Happen?

Language Objective
Answer questions about events in U.S. history from a time line prompt.

Use the time line on the left to answer the following questions. Answer in complete sentences.

1775 ——— 1775 U.S. Revolutionary War against Britain started.

1780 └— 1776 Declaration of Independence. The U.S. declared itself free from Britain.

1785

1787 James Madison and others wrote the Constitution.

1790

1795 └— 1789 George Washington became the first U.S. President.

1800

1803 Thomas Jefferson bought the Louisiana Territory from Napoleon of France.

1805

1810

1812 War of 1812 started. U.S. lost early battles.

1815

1820 └— 1814 British army burned Washington, D.C. War of 1812 ended.

1825

1830

1835

1840

1845 ——— 1845 Texas joined the U.S.

1850 └— 1846 The Mexican War. U.S. fought against Mexico.

1855

1860 — 1861 The U.S. Civil War started. North fought against South.

1865 ——— 1865 The U.S. Civil War ended. The North won.

1870 └— 1869 Wyoming became the first state to give women the right to vote.

1875

1880

1885

1890

1895 ——— 1895 The Spanish-American War. U.S. fought against Spain.

1900

1. When did the Mexican War start?

_____

_____

3. What did Thomas Jefferson do in 1803?

_____

_____

4. When did the Spanish-American War start?

_____

_____

5. What happened in Wyoming in 1869?

_____

_____

6. When did Texas join the United States?

_____

_____

7. When did George Washington become President?

_____

_____

8. When did the United States declare independence from Britain?

_____

9. What happened in 1895?

_____

_____

10. When did U.S. politicians write the Constitution?

_____

_____

11. What happened in Washington, D.C., in 1814?

_____

_____

SKILL OBJECTIVES: Interpreting a time line; sequencing. Have volunteers read the notations on the time line aloud. Provide help with reading dates and with vocabulary, if necessary. Then go through the eleven questions orally, having students answer in complete sentences. If students have additional knowledge about any of the events or places, encourage discussion. Have students complete the page independently, writing their answers in complete sentences.

Dear Dot

Dear Dot

Dear Dot,
   Yesterday I didn't have to go to work. I cleaned my room and my roommate's room, too. I waxed the floor and emptied the baskets. I shortened one of my skirts and one of hers too. I cooked dinner, but Anna's burned by mistake. Now Anna is mad at me. Can you believe it? After I did all those things for her, she's mad at me. What can I do?

Jane

1. What did Jane do yesterday? _____

   _____

2. Why do you think Anna is mad at Jane? _____

   _____

3. Is Anna right to be mad at Jane? Why or why not? _____

   _____

4. What does the word *mad* mean in this letter? Circle the best answer.

   a. crazy   **b.** sad   **c.** angry   **d.** surprised

5. Write a letter to Jane. Tell her what you think she ought to do.

   Dear Jane, _____

   _____

   _____

   _____

   _____

   _____

   _____

   _____

SKILL OBJECTIVES: Reading comprehension; understanding words through context; making judgments; writing a letter. Have a volunteer read the letter aloud while the class follows along. Explain any unfamiliar vocabulary. Ask students to reread the letter silently and answer questions 1–4. Discuss their answers to questions 2 and 3. Then talk about what their advice to Jane would be, and have them take Dear Dot's role and write their replies.

64

Language Objective
Talk about picture prompts using irregular past tense verb forms.

Some verbs have irregular past forms. Look at the following examples.

I **had** a bad dream last night.	Kim **went** to Korea last year.
They **ate** lunch at school yesterday.	Tran **rang** the doorbell but no one answered.

A Use the Data Bank to find the correct irregular past tense verb for each picture. Write a sentence about the picture using that verb. The first one is done for you.

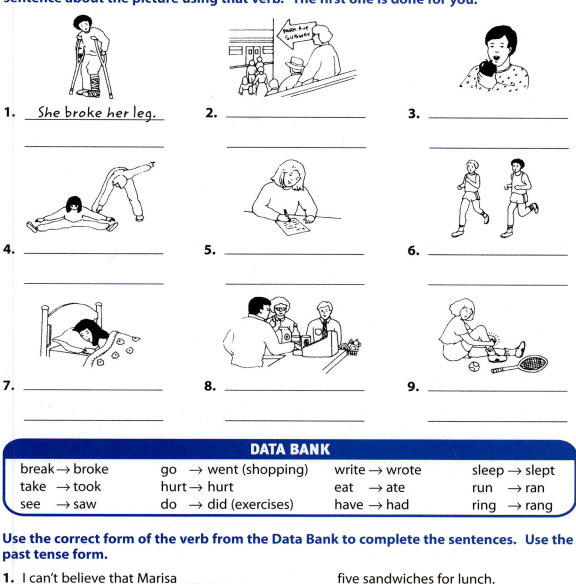

1. *She broke her leg.*

2. _____

3. _____

4. _____

5. _____

6. _____

7. _____

8. _____

9. _____

DATA BANK

break → broke	go → went (shopping)	write → wrote	sleep → slept
take → took	hurt → hurt	eat → ate	run → ran
see → saw	do → did (exercises)	have → had	ring → rang

B Use the correct form of the verb from the Data Bank to complete the sentences. Use the past tense form.

1. I can't believe that Marisa _____ five sandwiches for lunch.

2. A few days ago I _____ a good movie.

3. Elias _____ a bad headache yesterday.

4. Ana and Katarina _____ the bus to class yesterday.

SKILL OBJECTIVES: Using irregular past tense verbs; writing sentences. To prepare students for this page, ask, "What did you do yesterday?" They will probably use both regular and irregular past tense verbs in their replies. Write two columns on the board, headed "Regular" and "Irregular," listing in them the verbs the students used. After you have listed ten or more, call attention to the grammar box at the top of the page and the Data Bank at the bottom of Part A. *Part A:* Do the nine items orally first. Then have students use the verbs in the Data Bank to complete Parts A and B independently.

What's the Problem?

Solve the following problems. The first one is done for you.

Your Answer

1. Mr. Thompson was on vacation. He played six games of tennis every day for a week. How many games of tennis did he play?

    __42__ games

2. Peter didn't do well on his history test. He got only 30 questions right out of 50. What per cent of the questions did Peter get right?

    _____ %

3. Yesterday, Diana read 90 pages of her new book. Her book has 270 pages. What fraction of the book did Diana read yesterday?

    _____

4. Mrs. Lee baked a cake yesterday. She used $2\frac{1}{2}$ cups of flour, $1\frac{1}{4}$ cups of white sugar, and $\frac{1}{4}$ cup of butter. How many cups of ingredients did she use altogether?

    _____ cups

5. Anton worked on his checkbook yesterday. He had $500.48, but he had to pay four bills: $89.50, $85.02, $66.10, and $25.40. How much did he have after he paid the bills?

    _____

6. Roberto wanted to know his grade for the second term. He needed to find out the average of his tests. His marks were 96, 91, 80, and 61. What is the average of his four tests?

    _____

7. Six people had dinner in a restaurant. The total bill was $96.12. How much did each person have to pay if the six people shared the bill evenly?

    _____

8. Maria's American friend, Joanne, asked how much Maria weighed. "Fifty kilograms," answered Maria. Joanne didn't know that a kilogram equals 2.2 pounds. How much does Maria weigh in pounds?

    _____ pounds

9. An express train left Charlestown at 3:00. It arrived at Centerville at 8:00. The train traveled 50 m.p.h. for the entire trip. How far is Charlestown from Centerville?

    _____ miles

10. What is the odd number that is less than 60 but more than 50 and is divisible by 11 and 5?

    _____

11. A factor is a number that can be divided evenly into another number. List all the factors of 50 including 1 and 50.

    _____

12. A square root is a number which multiplied by itself gives another number. 4 is the square root of 16 ($4 \times 4 = 16$). What is the square root of 64?

    _____

SKILL OBJECTIVE: Solving mathematical word problems. Read the first problem aloud. Ask, "What do we want to find out? What facts do we know?" List the facts on the board: *6 games every day. Played 7 days.* Let students discuss what process should be used to solve the problem, then write the mathematical equation: $6 \times 7 =$ _____. Do the first three word problems as a group. Students who are comfortable with the skill can then complete the page independently. Continue to work closely with other students. Answers can be found on page 117.

The Present and Past of *to be*

Language Objective
Answer questions and write sentences using the correct tense of the verb <u>to be</u>.

Present	Past
I **am** happy.	I **was** happy.
She **is** sick.	She **was** sick.
He **is** a student.	He **was** a student.
It **is** sunny.	It **was** sunny.
You **are** tired.	You **were** tired.
We **are** late for class.	We **were** late for class.
They **are** in the kitchen.	They **were** in the kitchen.

A Look at the chart below. Then write sentences about each person. Use the past and present forms of the verb *to be*. The first one is done for you.

Person	Past Job	Years	Present Job
1. Eduardo	sales assistant	1996–2002	travel agent
2. Hamid	soccer player	1995–2000	TV sports commentator
3. Sasha and Luz	cashiers	1993–2004	store managers
4. Laura	computer programmer	1985–1998	college teacher
5. José	musician	2000–2003	disc jockey

1. _Eduardo was a sales assistant for six years. Now he is a travel agent._
2. _____
3. _____
4. _____
5. _____

B Answer these questions with short sentences. The first one is done for you.

1. Is Texas a state? _Yes, it is._
2. Were you in class yesterday? _____
3. Are you from China? _____
4. Was your teacher sick yesterday? _____
5. Was it sunny on Saturday? _____
6. Is your mother a doctor? _____
7. Are Boston and Miami states? _____
8. Were the streets wet this morning? _____

SKILL OBJECTIVES: Past tense of *to be*; comparing uses of the present and past tense. Teach/review the present and past forms of *to be*. *Part A:* Go through this as an oral group exercise before assigning it as independent written work. *Part B:* Do the first two items together, then have the students complete Part B independently.

Sally Ride

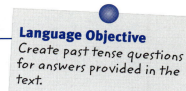
A Read the time outline about Sally Ride, the first American woman astronaut. Then write questions about her. The answer to each question is at the right. The question you write has to go with this answer. The first word of each question is at the left. The first question is done for you.

1951	Was born in California
1969	Graduated from high school
1973	Received two Bachelor's degrees (B.S. and B.A.) from Stanford University
1976	Got a Ph.D. in Physics
1977	Began astronaut training
1978	Applied to be an astronaut
1980	Became a jet pilot
1981	NASA chose Sally for the seventh *Challenger* shuttle flight
1982	Married Steve Hawley
1983	Became the first American woman to travel in space

1. Where ___was Sally born?___   She was born in California.

2. When _____?   She graduated from high school in 1969.

3. How many _____?   She received two Bachelor's degrees.

4. Where _____?   She got her Bachelor's degrees at Stanford University.

5. When _____?   She got her Ph.D. in 1976.

6. What _____?   Her major was physics.

7. Did _____?   Yes, she did.

8. How long ago _____?   She became a jet pilot _____ years ago.

9. What _____?   NASA is the National Aeronautics and Space Agency.

10. Who _____?   She married Steve Hawley.

11. When _____?   In 1983.

B The first woman astronaut to travel in space was not an American. Her name is Valentina Tereshkova. Using the Internet or an encyclopedia, find out where she is from and when she first went into space. In your notebook, write a short time outline about her based on your research.

An Unlucky Day

Language Objective
Talk about two actions that happened in the past using the simple past and the past progressive tenses.

The past progressive describes a continuing activity in the past. It is often used to describe something that was happening at the same time that something else happened. Look at the box for examples of the past progressive.

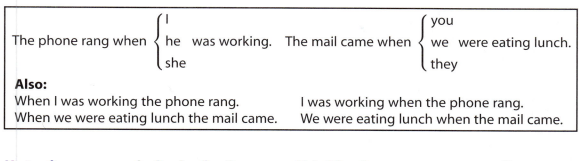

| The phone rang when | I / he / she was working. | The mail came when | you / we / they were eating lunch. |

Also:

When I was working the phone rang.   I was working when the phone rang.
When we were eating lunch the mail came. We were eating lunch when the mail came.

Yesterday was an unlucky day for George and his friends. Write what happened to everyone. The first one is done for you.

1. George

(cut) face; (shave)

He cut his face when he was shaving.

2. Sue

(hurt) arm; (play) tennis

_____

_____

3. Barbara and Carla

dog (chase); (run)

_____

_____

4. Tom

(find) fly; (eat) soup

_____

_____

5. Jill and Oscar

(hit) tree; (drive)

_____

_____

6. Pat

(burn) finger; (cook)

_____

_____

DATA BANK		
burn → burned	cut → cut	hit → hit
chase → chased	find → found	hurt → hurt

SKILL OBJECTIVE: Using the simple past and past progressive tenses. Teach/review the formation of the past progressive tense. Call attention to the example box at the top of the page. Have students note the relation between the two past actions: "The phone rang when he was working." The past progressive is an action going on, continuing, when the other (the past) takes place. Do the six items orally: "What happened to _____ when _____ was/were _____ ing?" After sufficient oral practice, have students complete the page in writing.

Tina's Terrible Trip

Language Objective
Write about two actions that happened in the past using the simple past and the past progressive.

Last winter Tina went to Miami for her vacation. She had a terrible time. Look at the picture story below.

Write sentences about Tina's trip. The first one is done for you. Use it as a model for the others.

1. (leave) house / suitcase (open) / clothes (fall) out

   When she was leaving her house, her suitcase opened and her clothes fell out.

2. (fly) to Miami / storm (begin)

   _____

3. (wait) for taxi / (rain)

   _____

4. (ride) to hotel / taxi (have) flat tire

   _____

5. (swim) / shark (follow) her

   _____

6. (play) tennis / (break) arm

   _____

7. (eat) in restaurant / waiter (spill) water on her

   _____

8. (sleep) / robber (break) into room and (steal) money

   _____

DATA BANK				
begin → began	break → broke	fall → fell	have → had	steal → stole

SKILL OBJECTIVE: Using the simple past and past progressive tenses. Teach/review the verbs used on the page. Pantomime the first picture to illustrate the idea of two past actions occurring at the same time, one an ongoing activity (past progressive) and the other a sudden occurrence. Draw attention to the signal word *when*. Do all eight sentences/pictures orally first. Encourage students to ask each other questions: "What happened to Tina when she was . . .?"

Susan B. Anthony: Fighting for People's Rights

A **Read Susan B. Anthony's biography. Then circle the best answer for each question.**

Susan B. Anthony lived from 1820 to 1906. During the 86 years of her life, she saw many problems in her country, the United States.

One of these problems was slavery. Susan B. Anthony grew up in Massachusetts, a state where people did not own slaves. But some states permitted people to own slaves. Susan B. Anthony thought all people should be free. Slavery was against everything she believed in. She wrote letters and gave speeches against slavery. Slavery ended in 1865 after the Civil War. But that did not end Susan B. Anthony's crusades against unjust laws.

Women had never had the right to vote in the United States. Susan B. Anthony and many others felt that women should have voting rights. In 1869 she helped start the National Woman Suffrage Association. This group worked hard to get women the right to vote.

In 1869, one state, Wyoming, gave women the right to vote. Some other states did too. But Susan B. Anthony and the National Woman Suffrage Association wanted all women to have the right to vote. They worked to add an amendment to the Constitution of the United States. In 1920, fourteen years after Susan B. Anthony's death, the 19th Amendment was added to the Constitution. It gave the right to vote to women who are citizens of the United States of America.

During the 1980s, Susan B. Anthony's picture was put on a U.S. dollar coin to honor her struggle for justice.

1. What did Susan B. Anthony think about her country?
   a. It had no problems.
   b. It had unjust laws.
   c. It was fair to slaves.
   d. It was fair to women.

2. What did Susan B. Anthony do about slavery?
   a. She permitted people to own slaves.
   b. She wrote and spoke against slavery.
   c. She started the Civil War.
   d. She had many slaves.

3. What does "suffrage" probably mean?
   a. the right to vote
   b. slavery
   c. pain and discomfort
   d. the right to fight

4. Which of the following is true?
   a. In 1870, no American woman could vote in an election.
   b. In 1869 states gave women the right to vote in some elections.
   c. Susan B. Anthony had the right to vote in all elections.
   d. Some states gave women the right to vote before 1920.

5. How did women finally get the right to vote in the United States?
   a. The Civil War gave them the right to vote.
   b. An amendment to the Constitution gave them the right to vote.
   c. Susan B. Anthony gave them the right to vote.
   d. Women got the right to vote when they went to work.

B **Elizabeth Cady Stanton was another woman who fought for women's rights in the United States. Did she and Susan B. Anthony know each other? Search the Internet or look in an encyclopedia to find out more about her. Write a short essay about her life in your notebook.**

SKILL OBJECTIVES: **Reading a biography; making inferences; learning test-taking skills.** Read the biography aloud (or have students read it silently if you want this page to be a "test.") Go over new vocabulary such as *slavery* and *amendment*. *Part A:* Do the first question together before assigning Part A as independent work. *Part B:* Students will need an encyclopedia or access to the Internet. Help them, if necessary, or encourage them to ask the school librarian for help.

Feelings

Here are some words that describe how people feel. Make sure you know what each word means.

angry	nervous	embarrassed
surprised	bored	sad
jealous	frightened	
disappointed	proud	

Language Objectives
Tell how people are feeling through the use of context clues. Write a short essay that provides context clues to tell how a person was feeling.

A Read the paragraphs on this page and the next page. Decide what the person is probably feeling, and write the word in the blank. Be ready to explain your answers.

1. Tommy's parents were out for the evening. He was alone in the house. The telephone rang. No one was there when Tommy answered it. He thought he heard a noise downstairs. Outside, there was a storm. Tommy heard loud thunder and saw bright, flashing lightning. He locked the door of his room and tried to stay very quiet.

   1. Tommy was feeling

   _____

2. Lorenzo's dog Leal was missing. Every night after dinner Lorenzo went outside to look for his dog. He walked through the neighborhood and called, "Leal, Leal." One evening a police officer came to Lorenzo's house. He had Leal's collar, with Lorenzo's name and address on it. "I'm afraid your dog is dead," he told Lorenzo. "He was hit by a car." Lorenzo took the collar. He looked away from the police officer. He didn't say anything.

   2. Lorenzo was feeling

   _____

3. The Phillips High School was having an art contest. Lisa walked into the room where her paintings were. There was a blue ribbon on one of her pictures. She was the grand prize winner. The judges gave her a check for $50.00. Lisa's friends and family congratulated her.

   3. Lisa was feeling

   _____

4. Maria lives alone in New York City. Her parents live far away in San Juan, Puerto Rico. Maria didn't know it, but her parents were saving money so that they could come to visit her in New York. One night she heard a knock on the door. She looked through the peephole in the door and saw her parents standing in the hall.

   4. Maria was feeling

   _____

5. Mr. Johnson was at the supermarket. He was in line, and the cashier was ringing up his groceries. She said, "$41.82, please." Mr. Johnson reached into his pocket. He didn't have any money with him. He didn't have a check, either. Mr. Johnson couldn't pay for his groceries. His face turned red as he tried to explain the situation to the cashier.

   5. He was feeling

   _____

(Go on to the next page.)

SKILL OBJECTIVES: Interpreting characters' feelings; building vocabulary. Teach/review emotion vocabulary or have students find the words in dictionaries. Ask a volunteer to choose an emotion to pantomime. The class will try to guess the emotion. "Are you (bored)?" When the volunteer answers, "Yes, I am," ask, "Why are you (bored)?" Encourage the volunteer and members of the class to suggest reasons. If interest holds, cover all ten emotions in this manner. Read and complete the first item(s) on this page as a group, then assign pages 72 and 73 as independent written work.

6. Jane's boyfriend, Ray, told the same stories all the time. All he ever talked about was his baseball team. She heard the same stories over and over again. Yesterday Ray was telling about the time he hit a home run in the ninth inning. Jane heard the story five or six times that week.

6. Jane was feeling

_____

7. Michel woke up early. Today was his big day. He thought he was going to become the new supervisor. He put on his best suit. He arrived at work early. He waited all day for the news. Finally at 5:00, the boss came into his office. He said, "Michel, I want you to meet Mr. Dubois, the new supervisor."

7. Michel was feeling

_____

8. Ms. Chin asked the neighborhood boys not to play ball near her house. They never obeyed. Whenever she heard the ball hit the side of the house, she yelled at the boys and told them to go away. Yesterday the boys hit a ball through her window. There was broken glass everywhere. Ms. Chin said that she was going to call the police.

8. Ms. Chin was feeling

_____

9. Mr. Smith was at the doctor's office. The doctor was in her laboratory. She was looking at Mr. Smith's X-rays. Mr. Smith was sitting, waiting for the doctor to come out. All the time he was wondering, "Am I sick or am I all right?" He was biting his fingernails the whole time.

9. Mr. Smith was feeling

_____

10. There was a school dance at the gymnasium. Rita walked into the gym and saw her old boyfriend, Sammy. He was dancing with his new girlfriend, Pamela. They were laughing and having a good time. Rita watched them all evening long.

10. She was feeling

_____

B **Now write a paragraph about a time when you (or a friend or a made-up person) had one of these feelings.**

_____

_____

_____

_____

_____

_____

_____

_____

_____

SKILL OBJECTIVES: Interpreting characters' feelings; building vocabulary. See annotation on page 72. *Part B:* Encourage students to title their paragraph with the feeling they choose to describe: "Jealous" or "Feeling Proud." Remind students that they do not have to describe something that really happened, they can make up a situation, either realistic or fantastic. Have volunteers read their paragraphs aloud, without the title. The class can then guess how the character is feeling.

Dear Dot

Dear Dot,
   My girlfriend Suzy and I were watching a movie at my place last night. We were both tired because we had worked all day, and we wanted to stay in and relax. The movie wasn't very interesting, but Suzy wanted to watch it to the end anyway.
   You aren't going to believe what happened next. We fell asleep. It was 4:00 a.m. when we woke up! Now Suzy's parents are angry. They don't want us to see each other any more. What can we do?

                                                    Danny

1. Where were Danny and Suzy last night? _____

2. Why were they tired? _____

3. Why did they want to stay in? _____

4. What happened to Danny and Suzy last night? _____

_____

5. What time was it when they woke up? _____

6. Who is angry at Danny and Suzy? _____

_____

7. What does the word *relax* in this story mean? Circle the best answer.

   a. retire   **b.** sleep   **c.** spend   **d.** rest

8. What do you think Danny should do? Write your answer.

   Dear Danny,_____

   _____

   _____

   _____

   _____

                                        _____

SKILL OBJECTIVES: Reading comprehension; understanding words through context; making judgments; writing a letter. Have students read the letter independently and answer questions 1–7. Correct these questions as a class. Encourage lively discussion of students' advice to Danny before having them write their Dear Dot letters to him. *Extension Activity:* A popular song from the 1950s, "Wake Up, Little Suzy" by the Everly Brothers retells this same predicament. If you can find this recording, your students should enjoy it.

74

Language Objective
Provide information about a school schedule.

Look at Armando's school schedule. Then use it to finish the sentences. The first one is done for you.

| Name of Student | Armando Rodriguez | Grade | 9 | Homeroom | 133 |

	Day 1	Day 2	Day 3	Day 4	Day 5
Homeroom 7:30–7:40					⟶
7:44–8:29	U.S. History	U.S. History	U.S. History	U.S. History	U.S. History
8:33–9:18	English	English	English	English	English
9:22–10:07	Computer Literacy	Computer Literacy	Study Period	Study Period	Computer Literacy
10:11–10:56	Science	Science	Science	Science	Science
11:00–11:25 / 11:28–11:53	Math	Math	Math	Math	Math
11:56–12:21	Lunch	Lunch	Lunch	Lunch	Lunch
12:25–1:10	Physical Education	Study Period	Physical Education	Physical Education	Study Period
1:14–2:00	French	French	French	French	French

1. Armando is in the _____9th_____ grade.

2. His homeroom number is room _____.

3. Armando is in his homeroom every day from _____ to _____.
(time)

4. Armando is in his U.S. history class _____ days a week.

5. He is in computer literacy class _____ days a week.

6. His English class is from _____ to _____ every day.

7. He is in physical education _____ days a week.

8. His lunch time is _____ minutes.

9. His math class is _____ lunch.
before/after

10. His science class is _____ his computer literacy class.
before/after

11. His _____ class is the last class of the day.

SKILL OBJECTIVE: Interpreting a school schedule. Have students examine the schedule. Ask questions such as the following: "Whose schedule is this? When is Armando in (homeroom)? At what time does he go to (English) class? How many days a week does Armando have (computer literacy) class? When does Armando have (study period)? How long is a class period in Armando's school? How much time do students have between classes?" Encourage students to ask each other questions about the schedule. Assign the page for independent written work. Correct as a class.

Helen Keller

A Before you read the article, look at the Vocabulary Preview. Be sure that you know the meaning of each word. Use the dictionary. Some words have more than one meaning. The way the word is used in the article will help you decide the meaning you want. Write down the meanings of the words you are not sure of.

Vocabulary Preview

strength	_____	communicate	_____
blind	_____	manual	_____
deaf	_____	celebrate	_____
silent	_____	eventually	_____
immediately	_____	hero	_____

B Now read the article. Use the dictionary if there are other words that you are not sure about. Notice that the words from the Vocabulary Preview are underlined.

The story of Helen Keller is a story of love, strength, and heroism. Helen Keller was born in 1880. She became blind and deaf when she was a baby. For six years, she lived in a silent, lonely world. Her family loved her and tried to help her but they didn't know how. They wrote to the Perkins School for the Blind in Boston, Massachusetts. They asked the school to send a teacher for Helen.

Annie Sullivan took the train from Massachusetts to Alabama and met the Kellers. She began to work with Helen immediately. Annie Sullivan already knew how to communicate with deaf children. She took Helen's hand into her own and spelled words using the manual alphabet of the deaf.

Helen quickly learned to mimic Annie's hand signals, but for a long time she didn't understand that the letters spelled words and that the words had meanings. She thought that the moving fingers were a game that she and Annie Sullivan played for fun. Helen had only three senses instead of the five that most people have, so a game using the sense of touch was fun.

Time went on. For days, weeks, and months, Annie Sullivan spelled thousands of words into the hand of her little student. Still, Helen did not understand.

April 5 was the big day. Helen was at the pump getting some water and Annie Sullivan spelled the word W-A-T-E-R into the child's hand. Helen spelled the word W-A-T-E-R back to Annie Sullivan. At last, she understood that one sequence of hand motions meant "water." Helen began to touch other things. She wanted to know their names. Helen understood. Annie Sullivan called the family. She told them that Helen was finally able to communicate. After Helen learned the words "mother," and "baby," she touched Annie Sullivan. "What's your name?" she was asking. Annie spelled T-E-A-C-H-E-R. Everyone went into the house to celebrate this important day.

(Go on to the next page.)

SKILL OBJECTIVES: Reading a biography; building vocabulary; understanding regular and irregular past tense. Allow time for students to look up unfamiliar vocabulary words in the dictionary and choose the appropriate definition. Review the definitions together. If you wish, read the article aloud before asking students to read it silently.

Helen had much to learn. Annie Sullivan helped her to learn about the world. <u>Eventually</u>, Helen went to Radcliffe College and graduated with honors. After Helen learned English, she learned five other languages. Annie Sullivan was always with Helen to help her through her hard work.

Helen Keller told her story to people all over the world. She wanted others to know about the problems of the handicapped. Because of Helen Keller, many people began to understand the special needs of the handicapped. Helen Keller was a great woman and a <u>hero</u> to millions of people all over the world.

A play and then a movie, *The Miracle Worker*, was based on Helen Keller's life. The miracle was the way that two people, Helen and her teacher Annie, learned to communicate in spite of Helen's deafness and blindness.

C   Use a word from the Vocabulary Preview to complete each of these sentences.

1. John is going to _____ because he graduated from high school.

2. The students were _____ while they were taking the tests.

3. When the radio broke, the pilot wasn't able to _____ with the tower.

4. People who can't see at all are _____.

5. Mr. Jones rescued three children from a burning building; he's a _____.

D   Read these sentences. If the sentence is true, circle *T*. If it is false, circle *F*.

1.	Helen became blind and deaf when she was six years old.	T	F
2.	Helen's family didn't know how to help her.	T	F
3.	The Perkins School was in Alabama.	T	F
4.	The Kellers lived in Massachusetts.	T	F
5.	Annie Sullivan traveled by plane to meet Helen.	T	F
6.	Annie Sullivan began to work with Helen right away.	T	F
7.	Annie Sullivan talked to Helen with her hands.	T	F
8.	Helen did not know that Miss Sullivan was "talking to her."	T	F
9.	Helen thought that she and Miss Sullivan were playing a game.	T	F
10.	Annie Sullivan spelled about two hundred words into Helen's hand.	T	F
11.	The first word that Helen understood was "water."	T	F
12.	The Keller family had a big party on April 5.	T	F
13.	Helen went to Radcliffe College.	T	F
14.	When she was older, Helen learned five languages besides English.	T	F
15.	Everyone admired Helen Keller.	T	F
16.	A play and a movie were made about Helen and her teacher.	T	F

SKILL OBJECTIVES: Reading a biography; building vocabulary; understanding regular and irregular past tense. Students should complete the exercises on this page independently. *Extension Activities*: 1) Students can locate additional information about Helen Keller in their library. 2) Many sighted deaf people use American Sign Language. Your local library should have some good books about this language. Interested students should learn some of these signs and teach their classmates some new vocabulary in sign language and in English.

Combining Sentences

Look at the two sentences below:

    a. Tom is a student.
    b. Mary is a student.

These two sentences can be combined to make one sentence:

    Tom and Mary are students.

Combine the sets of sentences below to make one sentence from each set.

1. a. Kamala is from India.
    b. Krishnan is from India.

_____

2. a. Kamala is from the northern city of New Delhi.
    b. Krishnan is from the western city of Mumbai.

_____

_____

3. a. Kamala speaks Hindi.
    b. Krishnan speaks Konkani.

_____

4. a. There are 179 different languages in India.
    b. Many people in India have to use English in order to communicate with each other.

_____

_____

5. a. Kamala speaks English.
    b. Krishnan speaks English.

_____

6. a. Kamala met Krishnan at a university in Mumbai.
    b. They got married two years later.

_____

_____

7. a. Kamala doesn't speak Konkani.
    b. Krishnan doesn't speak Hindi.   (Note: Use *so* after 7b.)
    c. They use English as their common language.

_____

_____

Now read all seven of the sentences you have written to tell the story of Kamala and Krishnan.

SKILL OBJECTIVE: Combining sentences with *and, but,* and *so.* Use information about your students to illustrate ways of combining sentences with *and, but,* and *so.* Examples: *1. (Luis) is from Chile. 2. (Ana) is from Chile. 3. (Jean) is from Haiti. 4. (Carlos) lives five miles from school. 5. He takes the bus to school. 6. (Tai) lives two blocks from here. 7. She walks to school.* Help students combine different sentences with the appropriate conjunctions. Do the page as a group exercise before assigning as independent written work. The last part may also be a written activity.

In the Library

A **Ana Poleo wants a library card. Read the dialogue with a friend. One of you can be Ana. The other can be the librarian.**

ANA: Excuse me, I want to get a library card.

LIBRARIAN: Do you live here in town?

ANA: Yes, I do.

LIBRARIAN: Good. Now you will need to have some proof of where you live. A letter addressed to you will do. Or perhaps you have a school ID card. You can also get a letter from a teacher.

ANA: Does the card cost anything?

LIBRARIAN: No, it doesn't. But if you lose it, it costs $1.00 for a new one.

ANA: Thank you. I'll bring my ID card tomorrow.

MPL **MUNICIPAL PUBLIC LIBRARY**
extends borrowing privileges to:

Ana Poleo

23 Elm Street

Smithfield

Telephone 555-1234

21544001204520

B **Ana's library has all kinds of things in it. Look at the pictures. Use the Data Bank to write the name of each of the different things she can find there.**

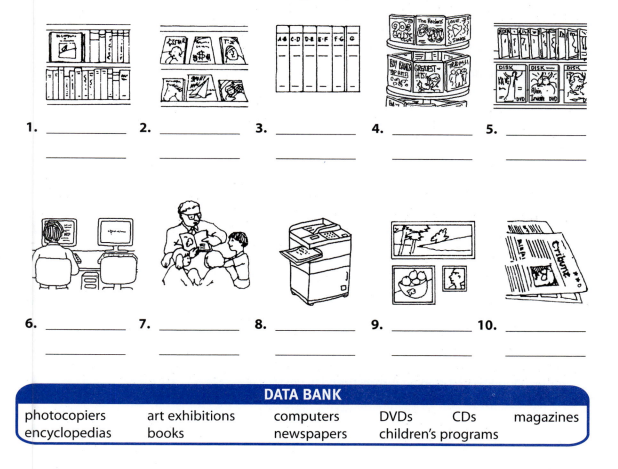

1. _____

2. _____

3. _____

4. _____

5. _____

6. _____

7. _____

8. _____

9. _____

10. _____

DATA BANK

photocopiers	art exhibitions	computers	DVDs	CDs	magazines
encyclopedias	books	newspapers	children's programs		

Don Roberts, Delivery Man

Language Objectives
Answer questions based on picture prompts. Write a short essay.

A Look at the pictures, then answer the questions that correspond to each picture. Work with a partner asking and answering the questions.

1. When did Don's alarm clock ring yesterday?

2. Where did he go after he got up?

3. What did he do there first?

4. and **5.** After that, what did he do?

6. What did he have for breakfast?

7. What did he do after breakfast?

8. When did he leave his apartment?

9. Did he walk or take the bus to the subway?

10. Why was Don running fast?

11. Why was Don upset?

12. While he was waiting for the next train, what did he do?

13. Why did his boss shout at him?

14. When Don went to his truck, what did he see?

15. Did Don have a good day yesterday?

B Write the story in paragraph form in your notebook. Begin with a topic sentence.

Example: Don Roberts had an interesting day yesterday.

C Work with a partner or small group. Study the pictures above for one minute. Close your book and try to recall as many pictures as possible. Let each person in the group have one or more turns as you try to recall all fifteen pictures.

SKILL OBJECTIVES: Reviewing past tense; telling a story from picture cues; writing a paragraph. *Part A:* This is an oral exercise. Have students examine the picture story. Introduce the character as Don Roberts. Have individual students contribute sentences to tell what happened in each frame. The story should be told in the past tense. When needed, ask questions about the pictures to guide the storyline and structure the verb tense. When all questions have been answered, have a volunteer tell the story to the class (or a partner) in his/her own words, using the questions/pictures as a guide. *Part B:* When students have had sufficient oral practice, ask them to write the story.

Choose the Verb Form

Language Objective
Complete sentences with the correct verb tense using adverbs and other context clues.

Present progressive	Simple past
Simple present	Future (*going to*)
Past progressive	

Use the correct form of the verb in each sentence. Look at the five examples. There is one for each of the five tenses in the box. Use them as a model for your answers.

Examples: (write)

Bob __is writing__ a letter now. (present progressive)

Bob __writes__ a letter to his family every day. (simple present)

Bob __wrote__ to his father yesterday. (simple past)

Bob __was writing__ to his family when the phone rang. (past progressive)

Bob __is going to write__ to his family next week. (future—*going to*)

1. (play)   Every Friday night my brothers _____ cards.

2. (take)   I _____ the bus to school every day.

3. (do)   Yoko _____ her homework now.

4. (take)   My class _____ a field trip next week.

5. (watch)   Yesterday Sasha _____ TV for five hours.

6. (ride)   Tomorrow I _____ my bicycle to school.

7. (drive)   At the moment, Mr. and Mrs. Pravdina _____ to Miami.

8. (snow)   It _____ when I arrived in Chicago.

9. (have)   Marisa _____ a math class at 1:15 every Tuesday.

10. (read)   Mr. Chin _____ a chemistry book when the lights went off.

11. (see)   Last night I _____ a good movie.

12. (go)   Nico _____ to college after he graduates from high school.

13. (find)   Mr. Rodriguez _____ ten dollars in the street yesterday.

14. (die)   Maria's dog _____ three days ago.

15. (play)   Rosita _____ tennis when it started to rain.

16. (take)   Next month Kim _____ a vacation in Tokyo.

17. (speak)   My sister and I _____ five languages.

18. (sleep)   Be quiet! The baby _____.

19. (cut)   Pat _____ her finger while she was slicing tomatoes.

20. (buy)   Henri and Claude _____ a new car every three years.

SKILL OBJECTIVE: Comparing uses of verb tenses: simple present and past, present and past progressive, and future (*going to*). Review the directions and examples with the students. Point out the spelling change in the example *write* (the silent *e* is dropped before adding *-ing*). For added oral practice, have a student pantomime running, singing, drawing, etc. and have students ask and answer questions about the action in all five verb tenses. Students can check the spelling of past tense verbs by referring to the lists on pages 65 and 69.

Helping You Study:
Alphabetical Order (4)

Many book titles begin with the word *A, An*, or *The*. When you put book titles in alphabetical order, you do not include these words. Instead, you alphabetize by the second word, and follow the regular rules of alphabetical order. If two titles have the same second word, alphabetize by the third word, and so on.

A Rewrite the following book titles in alphabetical order. The first one is done for you.

Title	Titles in Alphabetical Order
The Wind in the Willows	1. *The Adventures of Tom Sawyer*
A Tree Grows in Brooklyn	2. _____
The Call of the Wild	3. _____
An American Tragedy	4. _____
The Little Prince	5. _____
The Three Musketeers	6. _____
An Impossible Woman	7. _____
A Holiday for Murder	8. _____
A Farewell to Arms	9. _____
The Adventures of Tom Sawyer	10. _____

B Check your work with your teacher or with another student. When you are sure you are correct, rewrite the following titles in alphabetical order.

Title	Titles in Alphabetical Order
A Tale of Two Cities	1. _____
The Hat on the Bed	2. _____
The Sun Also Rises	3. _____
A Walk in the Dark	4. _____
An Old Friend from High School	5. _____
The Ice Age	6. _____
A Certain Slant of Light	7. _____
The Old Man and the Sea	8. _____
A Pocketful of Miracles	9. _____

SKILL OBJECTIVE: Alphabetizing book titles. Read the explanatory paragraph aloud. If you wish, have a student write the alphabet on the board for reference. Do several items in Part A with the class, then allow students to complete the exercise independently. Correct Part A together. Before assigning Part B, you may wish to write the following titles on the board for the class to alphabetize and discuss: *A Tale of Two Cities, Tale of Genji*, and *A Tangled Tale*. Let students complete Part B independently, then correct as a class.

Jesse James, a Famous Outlaw

Read the story.

Jesse James is one of the most famous outlaws in United States history. He robbed banks and trains from the late 1860s to the early 1880s.

Jesse James and his brothers fought for the South in the American Civil War. They did not fight in the regular army, though. The Jameses joined outlaw gangs that attacked Northern forces. When the South lost the war, the James brothers were angry. They started robbing Northern banks and railroads to show their hatred for the North. They also wanted money they didn't have to work for. They traveled with other outlaws, robbing and running away.

Most people were afraid of Jesse James. They thought he was a violent and dangerous man. Other people thought he was smart. For more than ten years, he and his brother, Frank, and the other members of their gang robbed banks and trains, and they always got away. Their luck did not last, though.

In the 1870s, some members of the gang finally got caught. Only Jesse and Frank escaped. The brothers decided to hide for a while. After three years, however, they and their new gang started to rob banks again.

The United States government offered a large reward to the person who killed Jesse James. Robert Ford, a new member of the James gang, wanted the reward. He shot and killed Jesse James in 1882. Sheriffs and policemen all over the country were relieved that the time of Jesse James and his gang was over.

A Now label each of the following sentences *Fact* or *Opinion*. The first two are done for you.

1. Jesse James robbed banks and trains. _Fact_

2. Jesse James was a hero. _Opinion_

3. Jesse James fought for the South in the Civil War. _____

4. United States criminals are the most violent in the world. _____

5. Jesse James was right to rob from the North. _____

6. Jesse James and his gang robbed banks and trains for many years. _____

7. The James brothers were cowards. _____

8. The James brothers hid from the police for three years. _____

9. Robert Ford killed Jesse James in 1882. _____

10. Robert Ford was wrong to kill Jesse James. _____

A Train Robbery

B Outlaws are people who think they are outside the law and are free to break the law. They may be considered heroes by people who share their ideas. Robin Hood is a legendary English outlaw of 800 years ago. Search the Internet or look in an encyclopedia to find out more about Robin Hood, and write a short essay about him. Tell why he is called "legendary."

SKILL OBJECTIVES: **Reading a biography; building vocabulary; distinguishing between fact and opinion.** Before reading the story (aloud or silently) introduce the concept of an outlaw. Students will want to talk about some "bad guys" they know from literature, television, the movies, or their own experiences. Go over new vocabulary such as *hero, gang, cowards*, etc. *Part A:* Before assigning the page for independent work, do the first two items orally to be sure students remember the difference between fact and opinion. If they are having problems, do all ten sentences together. *Part B:* Encourage use of the Internet, if available, or an encyclopedia to learn about Robin Hood.

Dear Dot

Dear Dot

Dear Dot,
   I am a Pisces. I was born on February 24. My girlfriend is a Capricorn. She was born in December. According to a book I have about horoscopes, Pisces and Capricorn are not a good combination. Pisces is romantic and artistic. Capricorn is serious and businesslike. We get along well now, but what about the future? Do you think that I have to break up with my girlfriend?

                                        Pisces

1. When was Pisces born? _____

2. When was his girlfriend born? _____

3. What does the book say about Pisces? _____

   _____

4. What does the book say about Capricorn? _____

   _____

5. What does the word *romantic* mean in his letter? Circle the best answer.

   a. sentimental   **b.** realistic   **c.** attractive   **d.** artistic

6. Write Dot's answer to Pisces. Tell him what he should do and should not do.

   Dear Pisces, _____

   _____

   _____

   _____

   _____

   _____

   _____

   _____

SKILL OBJECTIVES: **Reading comprehension; understanding words through context; making judgments; writing a letter.**
Teach/review the words *horoscope* and *astrology*. Have students read the letter independently and answer questions 1–5. Correct these questions as a class. Encourage discussion about what Dot should say to Pisces, then have students take Dot's role and write their advice to him. As an extension activity, have students bring in several different astrology columns for the same time period. Discuss why their predictions are so different for the same "sign."

84

Language Objective
Predict where an action is taking place based on context clues.

Imperatives are everywhere. Someone is always telling someone else what to do or what not to do. Read the commands below. Where are you if you hear someone say the following? The first answer is done for you.

1. "Pull in your stomach. Push out your chest. Keep your shoulders high. March, two, three, four. March, two, three, four."

   in the army

2. "Pay attention. Listen quietly. Don't talk and don't copy anyone else's paper."

   _____

3. "Take two of these every three hours. Drink a lot of liquids. Come back and see me in three days if you don't feel better."

   _____

4. "Don't get too close to the animals. Don't give them any food and don't tease them, please."

   _____

5. "Empty the trash. Wash the dishes. Play with your little brother. Be quiet."

   _____

6. "Fasten your seat belts. Don't smoke. Stay in your seats until we are off the ground."

   _____

7. "Put on your signal. Slow down. Take the turn. Give it some more gas. Keep going."

   _____

8. "Jump up and down. Stretch your arms out. Touch your toes. Don't bend your knees."

   _____

9. "Walk downstage. Take a deep breath. Look at the audience. Say your lines."

   _____

10. "Bend your knees a little. Dig your poles into the ground. Give yourself a little push and you're off."

    _____

DATA BANK

in an airplane	~~in the army~~	in a car	in a classroom
at the doctor's office	at exercise class	at home	at the zoo
on a mountain	in a theater		

SKILL OBJECTIVES: Recognizing imperatives; drawing conclusions. Read the introductory paragraph aloud. Explain the word *imperatives*. Read and solve the first one or two examples as a group, then assign the page for independent written work.

Opposites

Look at each numbered word. Find the opposite word in the Data Bank, and write it on the line. The first one is done for you.

1. beautiful _____ugly_____
2. never _____
3. married _____
4. boring _____
5. sick _____
6. worst _____
7. unfriendly _____
8. cheap _____
9. right _____
10. back _____
11. fast _____
12. difficult _____
13. answer _____
14. whispering _____
15. going _____
16. stupid _____

17. late _____
18. selling _____
19. forget _____
20. last _____
21. begin _____
22. arrive _____
23. withdraw _____
24. bottom _____
25. hated _____
26. evening _____
27. noisy _____
28. loser _____
29. shut _____
30. drying _____
31. safe _____
32. heavy _____

DATA BANK

always	end	leave	shouting
best	expensive	light	single
buying	first	loved	slow
coming	friendly	morning	top
dangerous	front	open	ugly
deposit	healthy	question	washing
early	intelligent	quiet	winner
easy	interesting	remember	wrong

SKILL OBJECTIVES: **Recognizing opposites; learning test-taking skills.** Read the directions aloud. Explain that striking out words in the Data Bank is a helpful test-taking technique. It reduces the number of answer choices for the next questions. Tell students to skip difficult items and complete the easy ones. Then they can return to the difficult items and choose the best answer from the few remaining choices. Do several items as a class, then assign the page for independent written work.

How Does It Work?

Most people use washing machines to clean their clothes, but many people don't know how a washing machine really works. Here is a short explanation.

Language Objectives
Answer questions about a reading. Put statements in the correct sequence. Explain a process.

A Washing Machine

A washing machine has many controls. You use the controls to turn the machine on, to select hot, cold, or warm water, and to set the time for the wash. When you turn the machine on, clean water comes in from the hot or cold water hoses. The water mixes with the detergent to clean the clothes in the drum. Water and detergent are not enough to clean the clothes. A motor in the washing machine pulls the agitator fins of the drum back and forth. The movement, water, and detergent clean the clothes. When the clothes are clean, a pump pushes the dirty water out through the dirty water hose. The motor spins the drum of the washing machine very fast. After the clothes spin for a few minutes, the washing machine turns itself off, and the clothes are ready to go in a clothes dryer or on a clothes line to dry.

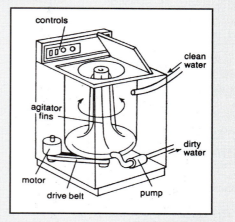

A **Read the article, look at the diagram, and answer the following questions. Circle your answers.**

1. According to the diagram, which of the following helps the motor turn the agitator fins?

   a. the clean water hoses   **b.** the drive belt   **c.** the pump

2. What happens while the clothes are spinning for the final few minutes?

   a. They get clean.   **b.** The motor rips them.   **c.** They become less wet.

3. Use the numbers 1 through 5 to show the sequence in which things happen when you wash your clothes in a washing machine.

   _____ Hot, cold, or warm water comes into a machine.

   _____ The washing machine turns itself off.

   _____ The motor pulls the agitator fins back and forth.

   _____ Turn on the machine at the controls.

   _____ The pump pushes out the dirty water.

B **Read about how a clothes dryer works. In your own words, write an explanation of the process, and draw a diagram of the important parts of a clothes dryer.**

SKILL OBJECTIVES: Reading a technical article; interpreting a diagram; making inferences; sequencing. Have students read the article silently. Tell them to look at the diagram as each part is mentioned. They may want to reread one or more times to be sure they understand how the washing machine works. *Part A:* Tell students that they are going to scan, or look quickly through the article, to find specific information that will help them answer the questions. *Part B:* Students can find information about clothes dryers on the Internet or in an encyclopedia. The school librarian can help them locate this information.

I Disagree!

David and Diane are twins, but they never agree about anything. If one says a certain day was cold, the other says it was hot. They always disagree. Look at David and Diane's statements below. Write what the other twin said on the line provided using a word from the Data Bank. Write your answer in a complete sentence. The first two are done for you.

Language Objective
Disagree with a statement by using an opposite word.

David

1. The boys were right.

2. _The glass was empty._

3. We were noisy.

4. _____

5. The tickets were expensive.

6. _____

7. The room was clean.

8. _____

9. It was sunny.

10. _____

11. The stories were wonderful.

12. _____

13. The dogs were huge.

14. _____

15. The animals were wild.

16. _____

17. His hair was straight.

18. _____

19. The sandwiches were thick.

20. _____

Diane

1. _The boys were wrong._

2. The glass was full.

3. _____

4. The store was open.

5. _____

6. He was guilty.

7. _____

8. The floor was wet.

9. _____

10. The bread was fresh.

11. _____

12. They were rich.

13. _____

14. The classes were interesting.

15. _____

16. The roads were dangerous.

17. _____

18. It was an odd number.

19. _____

20. The children were sick.

DATA BANK

tame	curly	thin	dirty	~~empty~~	healthy	terrible
dry	tiny	safe	cheap	even	rainy	boring
~~wrong~~	quiet	poor	closed	innocent	stale	

SKILL OBJECTIVES: Recognizing opposites; building vocabulary. As a warm-up activity, put a few words on the board such as *hot–cold, black–white, tall–_____, happy–_____.* Have volunteers fill in the blanks. Provide more examples if you wish to. Then read the directions aloud. To be sure students understand, try the first few items together. Call attention to the Data Bank. Tell students to skip difficult items and complete the easy ones. Then they can return to the difficult ones and use the Data Bank to figure out the few remaining choices. Assign the page for independent written work.

Helping You Study: Using the Card Catalog

Language Objective
Use a library card catalog to find books by title or author.

Read the following text.

Many libraries have a card catalog. There are cards in the catalog for all the books in the library. You can look in the card catalog and find the title or author of any book that the library owns.

The cards in the catalog are in alphabetical order. Authors are listed by last name. Titles are listed by first word except for *a*, *an*, and *the*.

The cards are in drawers. On the front of each drawer is a label. The label tells what cards are in the drawer.

Look at the picture of the card catalog drawers above. In which drawer would you find each of the following authors and titles? The first one is done for you.

The Gallant Five	5	*The Adventures of Ulysses*	
E. B. White		*Too Near the Sun*	
Rain or Shine		*A Fabulous Creature*	
The World of Animals		Shirley Jackson	
Ray Bradbury		*How to Fix Cars*	
Conquistadors		Agatha Christie	
Mark Twain		*Bright Candles*	
Never Is a Long, Long Time		Kurt Vonnegut	
Judy Blume		Norma Klein	

SKILL OBJECTIVE: Locating card catalog entries. Read the explanatory paragraphs aloud. Ask volunteers to name two authors and two book titles. Write these on the board. Help students decide in which card catalog drawer they would look to find each. Do one or two items together, then assign this page for independent work. *Extension Activity:* Discuss the types of books written by the authors listed here. Encourage students to choose an author to look up in the catalog of the library and read a short story or novel by that author.

Emergency!

A What do you do if someone you know accidentally swallows poison or pills? Read the list below and find out.

FIRST AID—POISON

1. Stay calm.
2. Look for the pill or poison container.
3. Call the emergency room of a hospital or the Poison Control Center.
4. Tell the health professional the name of the pill or poison and how much the victim swallowed.
5. Follow the directions of the health professional.
6. If they ask you to go to the hospital, bring the pill or poison container with you.
7. Do not give the victim any liquids unless the health professional tells you to.
8. Do not make the victim vomit unless the health professional tells you to.
9. Do not give any salt solution (salt mixed with any liquid).

B Use the information in the list to answer the following questions.

1. What is the first thing to do in a poisoning emergency?

_____

2. What do you do before you call the hospital or poison center?

_____

3. What information are you going to give the health professional?

_____

4. If you take the victim to the hospital, what are you going to bring with you?

_____

5. What two things are you not going to do unless the doctor tells you to?

_____

6. What is a salt solution? _____

7. What is a health professional? _____

SKILL OBJECTIVES: Following directions; using imperatives; understanding words through context. Have students read the emergency instructions silently, then name any unknown words. Let other students explain the words, or define them yourself. Go over some or all of the questions as a class, then assign for independent written work. *Extension Activity:* At home, have students copy directions printed on food containers, appliances, etc. As students read these directions aloud, their classmates can guess where they were written.

Which One Is Correct?

Language Objective
Complete a sentence by choosing the correct verb form.

Be careful with present tense verbs after *who* and *that*. Look at the following examples to help you to understand which form of the verb to use.

Singular	Dmetri is a boy who **likes** cake.
	The computer is a tool that **makes** work easy.
	This is the book that **tells** about fixing cars.
Plural	My friends are boys who **like** cake.
	Computers are tools that **make** work easy.
	These are the books that **tell** about fixing cars.

Now look at the following sentences. Choose the correct form of the verb according to the examples above and circle it. The first one is done for you.

1. Katya is a girl who (like / (likes)) to smile.

2. Those are the boys who (know / knows) the answer to the question.

3. José is an athlete who (run / runs) five miles every day.

4. New York is a city that (have / has) a lot of people.

5. Surgeons are doctors who (operate / operates) on people.

6. The Red Cross is an organization that (help / helps) people.

7. This is my cousin who (live / lives) in Baltimore.

8. Cats are animals that (sleep / sleeps) most of the day.

9. Mr. Podgorny is the man who (clean / cleans) our school.

10. This is the key that (lock / locks) the back door.

11. The mail carrier is the person who (deliver / delivers) the mail.

12. The office assistants (open / opens) the mail.

13. A photographer is a person who (take / takes) pictures.

14. Reporters are people who (write / writes) the news.

15. Tomás is a man who (speak / speaks) eight different languages.

16. A globetrotter is a person who (travel / travels) all around the world.

17. There are some whales that (weigh / weighs) more than sixty tons.

18. Electronics is a subject that (interest / interests) many people.

19. Kangaroos are animals that (carry / carries) their babies in pouches.

20. Florida is a state that (export / exports) a lot of fruit.

21. The eucalyptus is a tree that (grow / grows) mainly in Australia.

22. Ecuador and Peru are the countries that (lie / lies) to the south of Colombia.

23. Stars are heavenly bodies that (have / has) their own light and heat.

24. A mechanic is a person who (fix / fixes) cars.

25. Artists are men and women who (paint / paints) pictures.

SKILL OBJECTIVES: Reviewing simple present tense; using adjective clauses with *who* and *that*. Call attention to the examples at the top of the page. When the word that precedes *who* or *that* is singular, the verb that follows *who* or *that* is singular. When the word is plural, the verb is plural. Complete the first few sentences as an oral group activity. Then assign the page for independent written work.

Dear Dot

Dear Dot

Dear Dot,
    I couldn't understand any English last year. I studied hard, and now I can speak English pretty well. The problem is my family. Now that I can speak English, no one else in my family is learning it. They depend on me to translate all the time. At first I liked the practice and I liked to be so important. Now I am spending too much time doing my brothers' English homework and translating for the rest of my family at the doctor's office, the supermarket, and the bank. What can I do?

                                        Translator

1. How did Translator learn to speak English? _____

_____

2. Why did Translator like to translate at first? _____

_____

3. How does Translator help her brothers? _____

_____

4. Where does Translator help her family? _____

_____

5. What does the word *pretty* mean in this letter? Circle the best answer.

    a. beautiful   **b.** nice   **c.** fairly   **d.** not very

6. What is your advice to Translator? Write a letter telling her what you think she can do to solve her problem.

    _Dear Translator,_____

_____

_____

_____

_____

_____

SKILL OBJECTIVES: Reading comprehension; understanding words through context; making judgments; writing a letter.
Teach/review the phrase *depend on.* Have students read the letter independently and answer questions 1–5. Correct the answers as a class. Encourage discussion of what Dot's advice to Translator should be. Ask students if their families depend on them to translate. How do they feel about the situation? Finally, have them write letters to Translator giving her their advice.

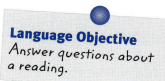

Language Objective
Answer questions about a reading.

Read the article.

The United States of America has fifty separate states united into one nation. Forty-eight of the states are between Canada and Mexico. The other two states are Alaska and Hawaii. Alaska is north of all the other states, on the northwest border of Canada. Hawaii is a group of islands in the Pacific Ocean. Alaska and Hawaii are the newest states. They became states in 1959.

Each of the first forty-eight states has a border that touches at least one other state. These two newest states are not even close to the others. How can they be united with them? The quick answer is all states are united by laws—the laws of the Constitution that rule and protect citizens of the United States.

The capital of the United States is Washington, D.C. Important federal government offices are in Washington, D.C. The Senate, the House of Representatives, the Supreme Court, the president and vice president work in Washington, D.C. All fifty states are represented there. Washington, D.C., is near the state of Virginia but it is not in any state. It is in the District of Columbia.

A **Now label each of the following sentences *Fact* or *Opinion*. The first one is done for you.**

1. Hawaii is one of the states in the United States.   _Fact_

2. Hawaii is the best place to live in the United States.   _____

3. Alaska and Hawaii are the newest states.   _____

4. All the states touch at least one other state.   _____

5. It is too cold to live in Alaska.   _____

6. Canada and Mexico have borders on at least one state.   _____

7. The fifty states are united by the laws of the Constitution.   _____

B **Read the passage again. Then look at the following sentences. Write *T* if the sentence is true, write *F* if it is false, and write *?* if the article does not give you that information. The first two are done for you.**

1. The United States of America is one nation.   _T_

2. Columbia in D.C. probably was chosen because Christopher Columbus sailed to the Americas in 1492.   _?_

3. The District of Columbia is in the state of Washington.   _____

4. The D.C. in Washington, D.C., means District of Columbia.   _____

5. Hawaii is one of the newest states.   _____

6. The United States has only forty-eight states.   _____

7. The Senate and the House of Representatives is in Virginia.   _____

SKILL OBJECTIVES: Reading for detail; distinguishing between fact and opinion; completing true/false/? statements. Teach/review any new or difficult vocabulary. Read the selection aloud and have students reread it silently. Tell them they can refer to it as often as they need to as they answer the questions. Do the first two examples in Parts A and B together before assigning the page for written work. Be sure students understand that the ? answer in Part B is used for any statement for which the passage does not provide information. (For example, item 2 may in fact be true or it may in fact be false, but there is nothing about it in the passage, so it is marked ?.)

A Map of the United States

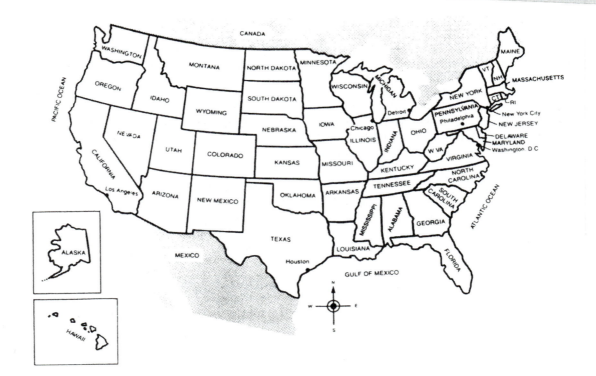

A **Use the map to answer these questions. Write short answers.**

1. Name five northern states.

_____ _____ _____ _____ _____

2. Name five southern states.

_____ _____ _____ _____ _____

3. Name five eastern states.

_____ _____ _____ _____ _____

4. Name three western states.

_____ _____ _____

5. Name five northeastern states.

_____ _____ _____ _____ _____

6. Name eight states that begin with the letter *M*.

_____ _____ _____ _____

_____ _____ _____ _____

(Go on to the next page.)

7. Name a city in Texas.

_____

8. Name a city in California.

_____

9. Name a city in Michigan.

_____

10. Name a city in Pennsylvania.

_____

11. Name a city in Illinois.

_____

12. Name the United States capital.

_____

B **Cross out the word that does not belong. Write the topic or category on the line above each group. The first one is done for you.**

1. _____states_____

Kansas

Utah

~~Los Angeles~~

Oklahoma

2. _____

Missouri

Chicago

Houston

Philadelphia

3. _____

Gulf of Mexico

Atlantic Ocean

Pacific Ocean

Canada

4. _____

Alaska

Hawaii

Puerto Rico

Virginia

5. _____

States

North

South

East

6. _____

Country

City

State

President

7. _____

Colorado

Ohio

Conneticut

California

8. _____

Iowa

Utah

Main

Ohio

C **What state do you live in? What do you know about it? Find the following information about your state on the Internet, in an encyclopedia or almanac, or by asking your teachers.**

1. Where is it located? (southeast? northwest? etc.)

2. What is the total state population?

3. What is the state capital?

4. What is the largest city in population?

5. Are there any mountains, deserts, volcanoes? Do earthquakes happen often?

6. What crops, products, or industries is your state famous for?

Write a paragraph about your state which includes the information you learned.

_____I live in_____

_____

_____

_____

_____

_____

_____

SKILL OBJECTIVES: Interpreting a political map; categorizing; learning/writing about a state. *Part B:* Discuss the first example and elicit that Los Angeles is crossed out because it is not a state as the others are. Have students complete items 2 through 8 individually or in pairs; discuss and correct them as a class. (Spelling is a factor in items 7 and 8.) *Part C:* Students can work individually or in small groups to find the information about their state. This could be an extended writing project which could include pictures or postcards. Students might choose to put their information into letter form instead of a simple paragraph.

The United States: a Geography Lesson

Language Objectives
Answer questions about a reading. Label features on a map from written information.

Read the article.

The United States is a large country with many different things to see and learn about.

There are long rivers and big lakes. The Mississippi River is a very big river in the central part of the country. It is 2,350 miles long, and it divides the country into the East and the West. The Great Lakes (Lake Superior, Lake Erie, Lake Huron, Lake Michigan, and Lake Ontario) are in the north. These are very large fresh-water lakes. They are important for transportation and industry.

There are two major groups of mountains in the United States. The Appalachian Mountains are in the East. They are very old mountains and not very high. The Rocky Mountains are in the West. They are quite large. Some are 14,000 feet high.

The middle of the United States, between these two mountain ranges, is a 1,500 mile plain. A plain is a large flat area of land with few trees. Many of this country's large farms are on this plain. A trip across the United States is an interesting experience. It is a lot of fun and a good lesson in geography.

A Now read these sentences. If the sentence is true, circle *T*. If the sentence is false, circle *F*.

1. The Mississippi River is 2,350 miles long.   T   F
2. There are six Great Lakes.   T   F
3. The Great Lakes are salt-water lakes.   T   F
4. The Rocky Mountains are in the West.   T   F
5. A plain is a group of mountains.   T   F

B What is this reading mostly about? Circle the best answer.

    a. the Great Lakes   **c.** the United States

    b. the Rocky Mountains   **d.** the Mississippi River

C Read the paragraphs at the top of the page again. Then label the features shown on the map of the mid-continental United States below.

SKILL OBJECTIVES: Identifying main idea and details; interpreting a topographic map. Read the article aloud. Teach/discuss any new or difficult vocabulary. Have students reread the article silently, then complete the three Parts independently. Correct and discuss their answers as a class.

96

Travels with Charley

Read the article.

John Steinbeck is one of America's greatest writers. Many of his novels and short stories are about people with troubles and problems. *Travels With Charley* is different; it's a book about traveling around the United States. John Steinbeck and Charley traveled together from New York to Maine and then to the Midwest. From the Midwest, they went west to California. On their way back east, they visited Texas. Finally, John and Charley traveled through the South, and back up north to New York.

John Steinbeck's journey took three months to complete. When he got home, he wrote about what he saw when he crossed the country. He decided that Americans were wonderful people, and that the United States was full of peaceful towns, great cities, and beautiful parks. Charley seemed to enjoy the trip, although he didn't say or write anything. You might wonder why Charley had no ideas about America. The reason is: he was John Steinbeck's dog, a big black-blue French poodle.

A Now answer the following questions. Circle your answers.

1. John Steinbeck started and ended his trip in

   a. California.   **b.** Maine.   **c.** the Midwest.   **d.** New York.

2. What did Steinbeck do when he returned from his trip?

   a. He wrote about what he had seen.   **c.** He got married.

   b. He stopped writing.   **d.** He decided he would never travel again.

3. The reading says that John Steinbeck's journey took three months. A journey is

   a. a trip.   **b.** a journal.   **c.** a country.   **d.** a novel.

4. Many of John Steinbeck's books and stories are about

   a. adventures on the sea.   **c.** teenagers in the city.

   b. people with troubles or problems.   **d.** life in the Old West.

5. What is a likely reason for Steinbeck's trip?

   a. He liked Charley.

   b. He wanted to eat good food.

   c. He like finding out about people's lives across the country.

   d. He wanted to write another novel.

B Use the Internet or an encyclopedia to find out where and when John Steinbeck was born, where he went to school, the names of his famous books, a brief summary of one of his books, any prizes and awards he won, and where and when he died. Use this information to write a short essay in your notebook.

SKILL OBJECTIVES: Reading for details; making inferences; learning test-taking skills. Tell students that this article is about someone who traveled through the United States. Read the article aloud, then have students reread it silently. Suggest that they follow the author's route on the map on page 94. You may want to show a copy of *Travels With Charley* to the students and let them browse through it after they have completed this page. *Part A:* Have students complete the five items independently or in pairs. Discuss the answers after they have finished. *Part B:* The school librarian can help students find information on Steinbeck.

Street Directions

Language Objectives
Answer questions about a map.
Listen to and give directions to
specific locations.

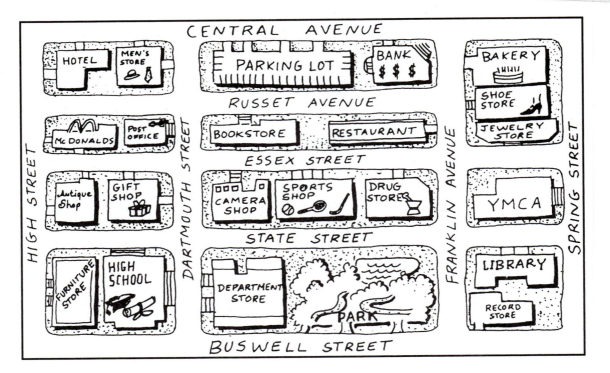

A **Read the directions. Trace the path on the map. Then answer the questions.**

1. You are in the park. Walk up Franklin Avenue and take a left on to Essex Street. Walk into the store between the camera shop and the drug store.

   a. Where are you? _____

   b. What can you buy there? _____

2. You are in the bakery. Walk down Franklin Avenue and take a right on to State Street. Walk one block, then take a left on to Dartmouth Street. You are in the building across from the high school.

   a. Where are you? _____

   b. What can you buy there? _____

3. You are coming out of McDonald's. Walk down Essex Street until you come to Franklin Avenue, then take a right. Follow Franklin Avenue to the end, to Buswell Street. You are at the store at the corner of Buswell and Franklin.

   a. Where are you? _____

   b. What can you buy there? _____

4. You are in the furniture store. Walk two blocks up High Street and take a right onto Russet Avenue. Go to the end of Russet and enter the store next to the bakery.

   a. Where are you? _____

   b. What can you buy there? _____

(Go on to the next page.)

B **Look at the map on the facing page. Read the problems below. Study the map, then write the street directions. The words in the Data Bank will help you. The first problem is done for you.**

1. You are shopping at the department store and you want to go back to your hotel. How do you get from the department store to the hotel?

    Walk up Dartmouth Street to Russet Avenue. Take a left on Russet

    Avenue, and the hotel is next to the men's store.

2. Susan is staying at the hotel. She wants to visit the jewelry store. How can she get there?

    _____

    _____

3. How do you get from the library to the post office?

    _____

    _____

4. How do you get from the bakery to the high school?

    _____

    _____

5. You're at McDonald's and you want to go to the park. How do you get there?

    _____

    _____

DATA BANK			
at the corner	on the left/right	next to	take a left/right
walk down	walk up	walk two blocks	between

C **Answer these questions. Refer to the map if you need to. Use short answers. The first one is done for you.**

1. Is the high school across from the bank? _No, it isn't._

2. Is the sports shop near the park? _____

3. Does a bakery sell fruit? _____

4. Can you buy film in a record store? _____

5. Can you buy shoes at a library? _____

Helping You Study: What Kind of Book?

Language Objective
Learn to classify books into the proper category.

We can divide the books in the library into three basic groups: fiction, non-fiction, and biography. Read the definitions of these basic groups.

Fiction	Stories that come from an author's imagination. Novels, mysteries, love stories, and space adventures are all works of fiction.
Non-fiction	Factual books about science, geography, history, mathematics, art, and medicine are works of non-fiction.
Biography	The life story of a person, usually a famous person. An autobiography is a book in which one person, usually someone famous, tells his or her own life story.

Sometimes you can decide if a book is fiction, non-fiction, or biography by looking at the title and author. Look at the following list. Write the name of the group in which each book belongs. The first one is done for you.

1. *George Washington* by James Flexner   _biography_

2. *The Age of Electronics* by C. F. T. Overhage   _____

3. *The Story of My Life* by Helen Keller   _____

4. *100 Years of Baseball* by Lee Allen   _____

5. *Mahatma Gandhi* by Vincent Sheehan   _____

6. *The Mystery of the Blue Train* by Agatha Christie   _____

7. *Mao Tse Tung* by Stephen Ulhalley   _____

8. *The Champion's Guide to Bowling* by Dick Weber   _____

9. *Mystery of the Haunted House* by Mary Bonner   _____

10. *The Last Days of Martin Luther King* by Jim Bishop   _____

11. *Journey Beyond Tomorrow* by Robert Sheckley   _____

12. *Let's Get Well* by Adele Davis   _____

13. *Space War Blues* by Richard Lupoff   _____

14. *My Life* by Bill Clinton   _____

15. *Radio's Golden Age* by Frank Buxton   _____

16. *Love and Mary Ann* by Catherine Cookson   _____

SKILL OBJECTIVE: Understanding library classification. Allow time for students to read the introductory paragraphs silently. Explain any difficult or unfamiliar words. Classify several items as an oral group activity, then assign the page as independent work.

What Were They Doing?

Language Objective
Tell what people were doing through context clues.

Read each of the following stories. Tell what the people were doing.

1. Liem drove into the driveway. The back seat of his car was full of paper bags filled with food, soda, detergent, and other household items.

   What was he doing?   *He was shopping for groceries.*

2. It was a hot day. Marguerite put down her brush. Her hair and clothes had little spots of white on them. She went into the house to get a cool drink before continuing her work.

   What was she doing? _____

3. Billy's father came into his room. He told him, "It's late at night. Go to sleep." He took away Billy's flashlight and book.

   What was Billy doing? _____

4. Rudy and Donna were very happy as they came into the house. "Look at these four big ones we caught!" they said. "We can make a delicious supper out of them."

   What were they doing? _____

5. Roberto was greasy and dirty. He look tired, but he was happy. "I don't have to walk to the office tomorrow," he said. "I finally got it to work."

   What was Roberto doing? _____

6. Sandra counted the words on the page. There were 250 words. Her teacher said, "That's very good work for five minutes. You are going to be a great secretary."

   What was Sandra doing? _____

7. Mrs. Lopez came into the house. Her hands were wet. She said to her husband, "Everything in the garden was dying of thirst. Luz didn't do any of her yard chores while we were on vacation."

   What was Mrs. Lopez doing? _____

8. René and Jules were soaking wet. They put away the pet shampoo and the special towel they used for Spot. "Well, he growled and barked a lot, but he's finally clean," said René.

   What were the boys doing? _____

9. Mr. Yu put away the dustpan and broom. He threw the glass into the waste basket. "I'm glad I got that broken bottle before any of the children stepped on it," he told his wife.

   What was Mr. Yu doing? _____

10. Mrs. Hernandez put down her red pencil. "That's the last one," she said to her husband. "Most of the students did very well. There were more than eight students who got A's, and only two who got F's."

    What was Mrs. Hernandez doing _____

SKILL OBJECTIVES: Using the past progressive tense; drawing conclusions. Do the first three items together as a group.
If students are having difficulty you may wish to do the entire page orally before assigning it for independent written work.

101

Dear Dot

Dear Dot,
   I have a question. I asked my sister Matilda to let me wear her blue dress to the school dance. Matilda's clothes are so pretty, and I wanted to look nice. That night at the dance, Max Dvoracek spilled coffee on me. It was an accident. Unfortunately, the coffee stained the dress and ruined it. Matilda says it is my fault. I say it is Max's fault. Whose fault is it? Whose responsibility is it to buy Matilda a new dress?
                                                Innocent

1. Why did Innocent want to wear Matilda's dress? _____

_____

2. What happened at the dance? _____

_____

3. What did the accident do to Matilda's dress? _____

_____

4. What does the word *innocent* at the end of this letter mean? Circle the best answer.

   a. not ready   **b.** not happy   **c.** not guilty   **d.** not free

5. Discuss Innocent's letter with your classmates and decide who is responsible. Then write a letter telling Innocent what you think she should do and should not do.

   Dear Innocent, _____

_____

_____

_____

_____

_____

_____

_____

                                    _____

SKILL OBJECTIVES: Reading comprehension; understanding words through context; making judgments; writing a letter. Have students read the letter silently, then independently complete questions 1–4. Correct these as a class. Encourage lively discussion of the proper advice to give Innocent, then have students write their letters giving her their advice.

102

Language Objective
Interpret a weather map to
answer questions about
weather in different cities.

A **Look at the map below. Write today's weather for each city.**

1. Miami   *It's hot and sunny in Miami. It's about 90°.*

2. Seattle   _____

3. Los Angeles   _____

4. Chicago   _____

5. Houston   _____

6. New York   _____

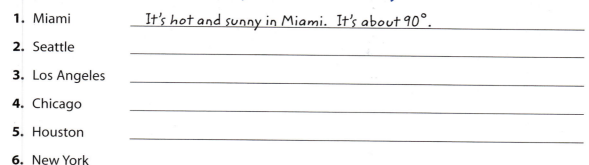

B **What's tomorrow's weather? Look at the chart below and write a weather report for tomorrow in the same cities.**

70°	20°	60°	50°	90°	15°
Miami	Seattle	Los Angeles	Chicago	Houston	New York

It's going to be cloudy and warm in Miami tomorrow, about 70°.

_____

_____

_____

_____

_____

_____

SKILL OBJECTIVES: Reading a weather map; using Fahrenheit temperatures; reviewing weather vocabulary. *Part A:* Discuss the weather map and review the vocabulary. If your students are unaccustomed to thinking of temperature in Fahrenheit degrees, call attention to the Fahrenheit scale at the right and tell them that this is the usual way of talking about temperature in the United States. Review the vocabulary and assign for independent work. *Part B:* This asks students to use the "be going to" future form. Do a few examples before assigning Part B as written work. As an extension, students may wish to write an imaginary weather report for their area.

What's the Temperature?

Average Temperatures (in Fahrenheit)

Place	January (Winter)	April (Spring)	July (Summer)	October (Fall)
Miami, FL	67°	75°	82°	77°
Houston, TX	52°	69°	83°	70°
Los Angeles, CA	54°	58°	68°	65°
San Francisco, CA	48°	55°	62°	61°
St. Paul, MN	12°	45°	71°	50°
St. Louis, MO	31°	56°	78°	59°
Cleveland, OH	26°	48°	71°	41°
Juneau, AK	23°	38°	55°	41°
Honolulu, HI	72°	74°	80°	78°
New York, NY	32°	52°	76°	47°
Washington, DC	35°	56°	78°	59°
Chicago, IL	22°	48°	71°	53°

Fahrenheit Scale

- 100° hot
- 80° warm
- 60° cool
- 40° cold
- 20° very cold
- 0°

° = degrees

A Look at the chart and the diagram. For each statement below, write *T* if it is true, write *F* if it is false, and write *?* if the chart and diagram do not give you enough information. The first two are done for you.

1. The coldest January temperature is in St. Paul, Minnesota. ____T____

2. It is windy in Chicago in January. ____?____

3. The temperature in Honolulu doesn't change much during the year. _____

4. It is hot in Juneau, Alaska, in July. _____

5. The yearly temperature in New York City varies from 32° to 76°. _____

6. There is a lot of snow in St. Louis, Missouri, in January. _____

7. Summers in Miami, Houston, and Honolulu have temperatures in the 80s. _____

8. A cool place to be in the summer is Cleveland, Ohio. _____

9. Temperatures often reach 100° in the summer in Washington, D.C. _____

10. Temperatures in October in Los Angeles and New York are about the same. _____

B The chart shows average temperatures. To compute the average of something, you add the numbers and divide by the number of items.

Example: Add 67 + 48 + 32. The total is 147. Divide the total, 147, by 3. The average is 49.

Now compute these average temperatures.

1. Jan. 4th, 31°; Jan. 11th, 17°; Jan. 18th, 25°; Jan. 25th, 8°. Average: _____

2. July 2nd, 78°; July 9th, 98°; July 16th, 83°; July 23rd, 91°. Average: _____

3. Oct. 5th, 71°; Oct. 13th, 66°; Oct. 20, 80°; Oct. 30th, 76°. Average: _____

SKILL OBJECTIVE: Reading and computing Fahrenheit temperatures. Discuss the chart of temperatures; refer students to the Fahrenheit scale and discuss the words *warm* and *cool*; compare them with *hot* and *cold*. Ask questions such as "What is the average temperature in Miami in January? Is that warm or cold?" or "You're going to visit New York in January. What kind of clothes should you take?" *Part A:* Have students complete the items individually. *Part B:* Be sure students know how to compute averages; provide several more examples before assigning Part B.

Thomas Paine

Read the article.

Thomas Paine made many important contributions to American history. He was born in 1737 in England. Although he was English by birth, Paine lived in Philadelphia for many years. He came to Philadelphia at the urging of Benjamin Franklin, an important patriot living there.

During his life, Paine wrote many pamphlets. Some of the pamphlets were published during the American Revolution. Because of their passionate support of the American cause, the pamphlets were very encouraging to American soldiers.

While in Philadelphia, Paine wrote a pamphlet called *Common Sense,* which stated that America should be independent from Britain. Another series of pamphlets he wrote was called *The Crisis.* These pamphlets were published between 1776 and 1783. The first of those pamphlets began with Paine's most famous line: "These are the times that try men's souls." He was talking about the Revolution, and how it tested the courage and dedication of the soldiers and the people of America.

Paine left America in 1787 to live in England and France. He died in 1809, back in America.

A **Now answer the following questions. Circle the best answer.**

1. Which of the following is true of Thomas Paine?
   a. He was a happy person.
   b. He lived his entire life in England.
   c. He wrote several influential pamphlets.
   d. He did not think America should be independent.

2. What was the main idea of *Common Sense*?
   a. America should be independent from England.
   b. England should impose lower taxes on colonists.
   c. Paine wanted to be a soldier.
   d. Paine did not like Benjamin Franklin.

3. The sentence "These are the times that try men's souls" comes from
   a. the Declaration of Independence.
   b. the Constitution.
   c. the Bill of Rights.
   d. *The Crisis.*

4. Why were the pamphlets Paine wrote encouraging?
   a. They were very funny.
   b. They were very well written.
   c. They were nicely printed.
   d. They passionately supported the American cause.

5. Paine died in
   a. England.
   b. France.
   c. America.
   d. Russia.

SKILL OBJECTIVES: Reading a biography; reading for detail; making inferences; learning test-taking skills. Ask students to name some important men or women in American history. Find out if they know anything about Thomas Paine. Before reading the passage silently, have students scan it for new vocabulary; help them to work out the meanings from context, if possible. After they have read the passage, go through item 1 with them as a class, then assign the remaining items for independent work.

The United States Government

A Before you read the article, look at the Vocabulary Preview.
Be sure that you know the meaning of each word. Use the dictionary. Some words have more than one meaning. The way the word is used in the article will help you decide the meaning you want. Write down the meanings of the words you are not sure of.

Vocabulary Preview

government	_____	representatives	_____
fair	_____	voters	_____
efficient	_____	elect	_____
power	_____	president	_____
branches (of government)	_____	vice president	_____
responsibilities	_____	courts	_____
laws	_____	protect	_____
follow	_____	rights	_____

B Now read the article. Use the dictionary if there are other words that you are not sure about. Notice that the words from the Vocabulary Preview are underlined.

The Constitution is the plan for the United States government. Important American leaders, including George Washington, James Madison, Alexander Hamilton, and Benjamin Franklin, wrote the Constitution in 1787. The writers wanted to build a fair and efficient government for the new nation. They wanted to be sure that no one person or group of people held all the power. So, they planned a government with three branches, or three separate parts. They divided the powers and responsibilities of government between these three branches.

The first branch of the United States government is the *legislative branch*. This is the branch that makes the laws. The second branch is the *executive branch*. This is the branch that carries out the laws. The third branch is the *judicial branch*. This is the branch that tells what the laws mean. It also makes sure that people follow the laws.

In the United States government, the legislative branch is the Congress. There are two parts of Congress, the Senate and the House of Representatives. The

men and women in the Senate are called senators. American voters choose them. Senators serve for six years. There are two senators for each state in the United States. There are fifty states, so this means that there are 100 senators.

The men and women in the House of Representatives are called representatives. American voters elect them also. They serve as representatives for two years. There are 435 representatives in Congress. States with many people have many representatives. States with few people have few representatives.

The president and vice president are in the executive branch. They have many thousands of people to help them carry out the laws and run the government. Americans elect the president and vice president every four years.

The judicial branch is the Supreme Court and other courts. The courts decide what a law means and if it follows the Constitution or not. All laws have to follow the Constitution. The courts make sure that people follow the laws. In this way they protect the rights of all Americans.

(Go on to the next page.)

SKILL OBJECTIVES: Reading comprehension; building vocabulary. Allow time for students to look up vocabulary words in the dictionary and choose the appropriate definition. Review the definitions together. If you wish, read the article aloud before asking students to read it silently. *Extension Activity*: After reading the article, ask students, "Who is the president of the U.S.? Who is the vice president? Are they Democrats or Republicans? When is the next election? Who are the state's senators? Who is the local representative?"

106

What is the main idea of this article? Circle the best answer.

a. The Constitution tells about the United States government.

b. The United States government has three branches, each with different responsibilities.

c. American voters elect the president, vice president, senators, and representatives.

d. The courts protect the rights of all Americans.

D **If the sentence is true, circle _T_. If the sentence is false, circle _F_.**

1. James Madison was one of the writers of the Constitution.   T   F

2. The Senate and the House of Representatives make up the Congress.   T   F

3. The states of Texas and Vermont each have two senators.   T   F

4. The president and vice president serve for four years.   T   F

5. The Supreme Court decides if a new law follows the plan of the Constitution.   T   F

E **Some words have several meanings. What does the underlined word mean in each of these sentences? Write the number of the definition in front of each sentence.**

Fair
1. not favoring one above another; honest
2. less than good, but better than poor
3. light in coloring
4. an outdoor exhibit of machinery, farm animals, etc.

_____ Her grades in school were only <u>fair</u> , but she was the star of the basketball team.

_____ Sweden has many <u>fair</u>-haired people.

_____ Do you think that the tax laws are fair?

_____ When my family goes to the <u>fair</u>, we eat hot dogs and ride the bumper cars.

Follow
1. to go or come after
2. to walk or drive along
3. to obey, to act in accordance with
4. to watch or observe closely

_____ Did that dog <u>follow</u> you home?

_____ The court decided that the law did not <u>follow</u> the guidelines of the Constitution.

_____ Did you <u>follow</u> the World Series?

_____ <u>Follow</u> Green Street two blocks, then turn left.

SKILL OBJECTIVES: Identifying main idea and details; choosing the appropriate definition. Students should complete the exercises on this page independently. Correct and discuss the answers as a class.

Helping You Study: Using an Index

Language Objective
Learn to use the index of a book to find information.

The index of a book is a list of all the main subjects, people, and ideas talked about in the book. The index tells you what page or pages to look at to find information about a subject. It is in alphabetical order. The index is usually on the last page or pages of the book.

Here is a sample index from a short book on early American history. Look at it. Then use it to answer the questions at the bottom of the page. The first one is done for you.

Adams, John, 219, 235
Articles of Confederation, 241–242
Aztecs, 40–43

Baltimore, Lord, 139–140
Boston Massacre, 206–207
Boston Tea Party, 210–211

Cabral, Pedro, 47
Cabot, John, 47
Canada, 46, 48
Cartier, Jacques, 46, 181
Columbus, Christopher, 24, 40

Dare, Virginia, 94
Declaration of Independence, 215
De Soto, Hernando, 83, 155

Franklin, Benjamin, 235, 249
French and Indian War, 192–193

George III, 202–203, 205

Hamilton, Alexander, 235, 244–246
Henry, Patrick, 235

Jamestown, 106–135
Jefferson, Thomas, 275

Lafayette, Marquis de, 228, 230
Louisiana, 185, 186

Mason-Dixon Line, 159–160
Mexico, 14, 40–45, 47, 178–179
Montezuma, 41, 43

Native Americans, 37–38, 101–102, 191–194
New England, 164–166

Penn, William, 153–155
Pilgrims, 145–148
Pizarro, Francisco, 41–42
Pocahontas, 122–123
Ponce de León, Juan, 101

Quakers, 155–159

Revere, Paul, 215–216
Revolutionary War, 214–234

Smith, John, 117–127
Stamp Act, 199–200

Vespucci, Amerigo, 39

Washington, George, 140, 219–220, 236–237, 244

On what page(s) is there information about:

1. Jacques Cartier   _46, 181_
2. Benjamin Franklin   _____
3. The Revolutionary War   _____
4. Alexander Hamilton   _____
5. Mexico   _____
6. Jamestown, Virginia   _____
7. Francisco Pizarro   _____
8. The Mason-Dixon Line   _____
9. The Articles of Confederation   _____
10. The Pilgrims   _____
11. Amerigo Vespucci   _____
12. Juan Ponce de León   _____
13. Marquis de Lafayette   _____
14. Virginia Dare   _____

SKILL OBJECTIVE: Using a book index. Read the explanatory paragraph aloud. Locate and discuss the answer to the first two questions as a class, then assign the page for independent work. *Extension Activity*: Have students work in pairs with the index of a science or social studies text book. Students should ask each other questions, "On what page(s) is there information about ...?" Both partners should then turn to those pages and see if they can locate the promised information.

Places and People

A **Use words from Data Bank A to complete each of the sentences. The first one is done for you.**

1. People play football in a _____ *stadium.* _____

2. People borrow books from a _____ .

3. Men and women play tennis on a _____ .

4. You can find a doctor in a _____ .

5. Children play baseball on a _____ .

6. People swim in a _____ .

7. You can buy nails in a _____ .

8. You play golf on a _____ .

DATA BANK A			
clinic	diamond	golf course	hardware store
library	pool	~~stadium~~	tennis court

B **Now do these sentences the same way. Use words from Data Bank B. The first one is done for you.**

1. A _____ *mail carrier* _____ is a person who delivers letters.

2. A _____ is a person who repairs sinks.

3. An _____ is a person who designs buildings.

4. A _____ is a person who sells meat.

5. A _____ is a person who tells funny jokes.

6. A _____ is a person who takes care of children.

7. An _____ is a person who writes books.

8. An _____ is a person who puts lights in your home.

DATA BANK B			
architect	author	babysitter	butcher
comedian	electrician	~~mail carrier~~	plumber

SKILL OBJECTIVES: Using *who* clauses; building vocabulary. Have students complete this page independently. Suggest that they use the test-taking technique described on page 86, completing the easy items first, striking out the answers, then returning to the difficult items and choosing among remaining answers. *Extension Activity*: Students can write completion exercises for their classmates: "A _____ is a person who ..." "A _____ is a place where ..." Additional location and occupation vocabulary can be found on pages 11, 22, 29, 88, 93, and 94.

Find the Ending

Match the beginning of each sentence with its ending. Write the letter of the ending in the blank. Be careful! Some sentences may have more than one possible "correct" ending, but you can use each letter only once. The first one is done for you.

1. A stadium is a place where ___*e*___

2. Libraries are places where _____

3. An astronaut is a person who _____

4. A zebra is an animal that _____

5. An encyclopedia is a set of books that _____

6. An ostrich is a large bird that _____

7. Mayors are people who _____

8. A governor is a person who _____

9. A skunk is an animal that _____

10. February is the month that _____

11. A restaurant is a place where _____

12. Movie stars are people who _____

13. Toyotas are cars that _____

14. Brazil is a country where _____

15. A saw is a tool that _____

16. Whales are large animals that _____

17. The 4th of July is a holiday that _____

18. Baseball is a sport that _____

19. Christopher Columbus is the man who _____

20. Tortillas are a food that _____

a. Portuguese is the official language.

b. has twenty-eight days.

c. people play in the summer and fall.

d. runs a state.

e. people play sports.

f. people use to cut wood.

g. travels in a rocket ship.

h. come from Japan.

i. contains lots of information.

j. live in the ocean.

k. cannot fly.

l. celebrates America's independence.

m. run cities.

n. comes from Mexico.

o. has black and white stripes.

p. sailed to the New World in 1942.

q. waiters and waitresses work.

r. make a lot of money.

s. smells awful when it is angry.

t. you can find books on all subjects.

SKILL OBJECTIVES: Reading comprehension; understanding adjective clauses with *who, where, what*. This exercise deliberately includes several possible completions for many of the sentence starters. The trick is to use each ending once. Remind the students to work in pencil as they may need to revise their answers several times. You may wish to let students work in pairs on this page.

110

Dear Dot

Dear Dot

Dear Dot,

    I am a girl who has a problem. I like a boy who works in a supermarket. He has to work until 10:00 every Friday and Saturday night. I have parents who are very strict and I have to be home at 10:00 on Friday and Saturday nights. I can't go out at all on school nights. I think you can understand my problem. I really like this boy but we only see each other at school. What can I do?

                                               Melissa

1. Where does Melissa's boyfriend work? _____

2. Until what time does he work every Friday and Saturday night _____

3. What rules do Melissa's parents have about her going out? _____

_____

4. When can Melissa and her boyfriend see each other? _____

_____

5. What does the word *strict* mean in this letter? Circle the best answer.

    a. tough   **b.** friendly   **c.** quiet   **d.** thin

6. What is your advice to Melissa? Write Dot's answer to her.

    Dear Melissa, _____

_____

_____

_____

_____

_____

                                       _____

SKILL OBJECTIVES: Reading comprehension; understanding words through context; making judgments; writing a letter. Have students read Melissa's letter independently and answer questions 1–5. Correct these items as a class. Then have students discuss what advice to give Melissa. Have any of them been in similar situations? How did they solve them? Finally, have each student write his or her advice to Melissa.

Vocabulary Review

Complete each sentence with a word from the Data Bank.

1. My _____ country is Vietnam.

2. Susan B. Anthony _____ a strong woman.

3. The mail carrier _____ the mail two hours ago.

4. Raoul's dog is sick; he's taking it to the _____

5. The police officer stopped the _____ so we could cross the street.

6. Thanksgiving is one of my favorite _____

7. _____ house is around the corner on the left.

8. Due to a storm the plane _____ two hours late.

9. I'm not sick at all; the doctor said I'm very _____.

10. Pierre _____ his bike six miles every day.

11. The boss _____ at me because I was late.

12. Mr. Salerno is _____ to lose some weight.

13. Several of my friends are _____ Chicago.

14. Alaska, Texas, and California are large _____.

15. It _____ snows in Hawaii.

16. You don't need a jacket; it's _____ out.

17. We were _____ bread when the telephone rang.

18. Gabriel dropped the glass and _____ it.

19. The boys _____ like painting or skiing.

20. Lions and tigers are _____ animals.

DATA BANK				
arrived	don't	Martin's	shouted	veterinarian
baking	from	native	states	warm
broke	healthy	never	traffic	was
delivered	holidays	rides	trying	wild

VOCABULARY REVIEW: The following four pages present a review of important vocabulary introduced at this level. You may wish to complete the first one or two items as a group, before assigning the page as independent written work.

Vocabulary Review

Complete each sentence with a word from the Data Bank.

1. Please write your _____ on the line.

2. I went to the bank to _____ my check.

3. Her secretary _____ the report yesterday.

4. The doctor saw twelve _____ in the last three hours.

5. The baskets are full of trash; please _____ them.

6. Javier _____ misses basketball practice.

7. Rebecca _____ a terrible toothache yesterday.

8. Did you ride in Kamal's _____?

9. Don't be late for your _____.

10. Mrs. Lee told a funny _____ at the party.

11. My sister is _____ her wedding for June.

12. We took a wonderful _____ in Colorado.

13. The nurse took my _____ and it was 99.5.

14. These books must _____ about twenty pounds!

15. Sammy got to class late because he had a _____ tire.

16. It started to rain when I was _____ the house.

17. Eduardo _____ all his shirts last night.

18. Miriam _____ when she is near a cat or dog.

19. The newspaper photographer _____ Leo's picture.

20. The pilot told the passengers to _____ their seatbelts.

DATA BANK

address	fasten	jeep	planning	took
appointment	flat	joke	seldom	typed
cash	had	painting	sneezes	vacation
empty	ironed	patients	temperature	weigh

Vocabulary Review

Complete each sentence with a word from the Data Bank.

1. Spring and fall are my favorite _____.

2. Maria wears beautiful _____.

3. The mechanic _____ our car last Tuesday.

4. A waitress _____ meals in a restaurant.

5. Please put your _____ on this line.

6. In an emergency it's important to stay _____.

7. I _____ go to the library to study.

8. The carpenter _____ have the tools he needs.

9. Pedro _____ weights at the gym every day.

10. Tina invited two hundred fifty people to her _____.

11. Gloria _____ Yale University last year.

12. Did you eat the _____ pizza?

13. Najeeb was feeling _____ after he watched a horror movie.

14. The weather in autumn is usually _____.

15. Let's drive; it's _____ far to walk to the museum.

16. Last winter we _____ on the frozen pond for hours.

17. Larry will work _____ when he graduates.

18. I was so tired that I _____ until 11:30.

19. We were _____ for the bus when the fire started.

20. The U.S. government has three separate _____.

DATA BANK				
attended	clothes	full-time	serves	too
branches	doesn't	lifts	signature	waiting
calm	fixed	often	skated	wedding
cool	frightened	seasons	slept	whole

VOCABULARY REVIEW: See annotation on page 112.

Vocabulary Review

Put the words from the Data Bank into the correct boxes.

Occupations	Feelings	*How Often* Words
1. _____	1. _____	1. _____
2. _____	2. _____	2. _____
3. _____	3. _____	3. _____
4. _____	4. _____	4. _____
5. _____	5. _____	5. _____

Irregular Verbs	Geography Words	Weather Words
1. _____	1. _____	1. _____
2. _____	2. _____	2. _____
3. _____	3. _____	3. _____
4. _____	4. _____	4. _____
5. _____	5. _____	5. _____

Law and Government	Money and Banking
1. _____	1. _____
2. _____	2. _____
3. _____	3. _____
4. _____	4. _____
5. _____	5. _____

DATA BANK

always	court	go	often	sometimes
angry	desert	interest	plain	sunny
break	deposit	jealous	proud	temperature
cashier	disappointed	lawyer	river	take
check	electrician	maid	representative	volcano
cloudy	embarrassed	model	savings account	vote
computer programmer	Fahrenheit	mountain	seldom	withdraw
Constitution	freezing	never	sleep	write

End of Book Test: Completing Familiar Structures

Circle the best answer.

Example: He _____ play soccer.

      a. (can)   **b.** is   **c.** knows   **d.** do

1. Ali _____ to work tonight.

    a. have   **b.** has   **c.** did   **d.** does

2. Do you like _____ Chinese food?

    a. eat   **b.** to eating   **c.** to eat   **d.** eats

3. _____ Mrs. Jones take the bus to work?

    a. Do   **b.** Is   **c.** Has   **d.** Does

4. My sister _____ the bus yesterday.

    a. is missing   **b.** miss   **c.** missed   **d.** misses

5. _____ you have chicken for dinner last night?

    a. Did   **b.** Do   **c.** Was   **d.** What

6. Where _____ you yesterday?

    a. were   **b.** was   **c.** did   **d.** are

7. _____ did the bus leave?

    a. That   **b.** When   **c.** Who's   **d.** How long

8. Marta didn't _____ her homework.

    a. finished   **b.** finishes   **c.** finish   **d.** finishing

9. I _____ when you called.

    a. slept   **b.** was slept   **c.** sleep   **d.** was sleeping

10. Reporters are people who _____ the news.

    a. write   **b.** writes   **c.** are write   **d.** writing

11. My teacher usually _____ papers in the evening.

    a. correct   **b.** correcting   **c.** corrects   **d.** are correct

12. My father _____ want to wash the dishes.

    a. don't   **b.** doesn't   **c.** do   **d.** isn't

Fannee Doolee's secret (page 7) Fannee likes words with double letters. She doesn't like words without double letters. Carlos likes words that end in -s.

END OF BOOK TEST: **Completing familiar structures.** The following testing pages will help you evaluate each student's strengths and weaknesses, and indicate his or her readiness to proceed to the next level of instruction. Review directions and examples with the class, then assign the pages as independent work. Remind students to try each answer choice in the blank space to determine which choice is correct.

End of Book Test: Completing Familiar Structures (continued)

13. How many hours _____ they work last week?

    a. does   **b.** can   **c.** did   **d.** do

14. Lidia cleans her room but her brothers _____.

    a. doesn't   **b.** don't   **c.** didn't   **d.** aren't

15. Hairdressers _____ hair.

    a. cut   **b.** cuts   **c.** to cut   **d.** cutting

16. Do you want _____ a movie?

    a. to seeing   **b.** see   **c.** seeing   **d.** to see

17. We're going to _____ favorite restaurant tonight.

    a. us   **b.** our   **c.** ours   **d.** we

18. Aziz doesn't _____ in class.

    a. listen   **b.** listens   **c.** listening   **d.** to listen

19. My teacher _____ to class early.

    a. seldom comes   **b.** comes seldom   **c.** seldom is coming   **d.** is seldom coming

20. When is your father going to visit you? _____.

    a. Last week   **b.** Two days ago   **c.** Yesterday   **d.** Tonight

21. Carlotta never _____ her exercises.

    a. is doing   **b.** to do   **c.** doing   **d.** does

22. Were you in New York last week? No, I _____.

    a. weren't   **b.** didn't   **c.** am not   **d.** was not

23. How many children _____?

    a. does Lucy has   **b.** has Lucy   **c.** does Lucy have   **d.** does have Lucy

24. How many years did Henry attend school? He _____ school for five years.

    a. did attend   **b.** was attending   **c.** attend   **d.** attended

25. My mother _____ lunch when I came home from school.

    a. make   **b.** was making   **c.** is making   **d.** makes

> **Answers to problems on page 66**
> **1.** 42; **2.** 60%; **3.** 1/3; **4.** 4 cups; **5.** $234.46; **6.** 82; **7.** $16.02; **8.** 110 pounds; **9.** 250 miles; **10.** 55; **11.** 1, 2, 5, 10, 25, 50; **12.** 8

End of Book Test: Writing Questions

Write the questions.

Example: William goes to school every day.

Where *does William go every day?*

1. Mary wants to be a veterinarian when she grows up.

What _____ ?

2. Mr. Bihiche works ten hours a day.

How many _____ ?

3. Mr. and Mrs. Carlson went to the baseball game yesterday.

Where _____ ?

4. Kathy washed her car yesterday.

What _____ ?

5. My brothers like to play the guitar.

What _____ ?

6. Jean and Paulo are going to college in two years.

When _____ ?

7. The bus comes at ten o'clock.

When _____ ?

8. Luz sleeps in the living room.

Where _____ ?

9. It rained yesterday.

When _____ ?

10. Peter was sleeping when I called him.

What _____ ?

11. Anton feels terrible.

How _____ ?

12. Susan paid $7,000 for her new car.

How much _____ ?

END OF BOOK TEST: Writing questions. Go over the directions and example with the class. Point out that the first word(s) of each question is/are provided. Assign the page as independent written work.

118

End of Book Test: Reading Comprehension

Read the story.

Graduation Day

Everyone in our family was very proud of Charles on Friday. He was graduating from high school.

The graduation ceremony was held in the auditorium of Cherry Brook High School at 7:30 p.m. . We went last year because Michelle, Charles' sister, was graduating. This year she came from California, where she goes to college, to see Charles graduate.

The ceremony last year was great fun, and this year it was no different. Everyone was so dressed up! I wore my nice jacket and some very shiny brown shoes. Michelle wore a pretty white dress. Charles had to wear a blue gown. Under it, though, he wore a black jacket, brown pants, and a yellow shirt. He looked sharp!

After a speech by the principal, Charles played the piano. Then another student sang a song from an opera. Some other students put on a skit. Then the students walked across the stage and accepted their diplomas. After the graduation ceremony, we came home and ate cake. Then it was way past my bedtime! What fun!

A **Now answer the following questions.**

1. Why was everyone proud of Charles on Friday? _____

_____

2. Where did the graduation ceremony take place? _____

_____

3. Who graduated last year? _____

4. Where did Michelle come from to see Charles graduate? _____

5. What did Charles's family do after the graduation ceremony? _____

_____

B **Number these statements in the correct order.**

_____ The students walked across the stage.

_____ Charles played the piano.

_____ The principal made a speech.

_____ Charles's family came home and had cake.

_____ Charles's family went to the high school.

What is this story mostly about? Circle the best answer.

a. Charles's piano playing

b. Charles's graduation

c. The principal of Charles's high school

d. Michelle's graduation

Index of Language Objectives

Agree or disagree
    about statements from a reading, 37
    with advice, 12, 21, 31, 43, 53, 64, 74, 84, 92, 102, 111
Answer questions, 67, 94–95
    about a map, 98, 99
    about a reading, 12, 15, 21, 24, 26, 31, 35, 4, 8, 43, 46, 51, 53, 60–61, 64, 71, 74, 76–77, 84, 87, 90, 92, 93, 96, 97, 102, 105, 106–107, 111
    about a Table of Contents, 11
    about daily activities using adverbs of frequency, 27
    about events in U.S. history from a time line prompt, 63
    based on picture prompts, 80
    career-related, using numbers and salary amounts, 40
    from a visual prompt, 25
    in past tense using specific dates, 59
    personal and general information, 2
    to state likes and dislikes, 6
    using possessive nouns, 36
Apply adverbs of frequency to specific statements, 23
Approximate where to find words in a dictionary, 30
Arrange words in alphabetical order, 19, 20
Ask questions
    about someone's daily routine, 32
    using correct form of do, 38
Associate
    common vocabulary words, 3
    sets of nouns with specific locations, 50

Categorize words according to specific titles, 115
Complete
    a sentence by choosing correct verb form, 91
    a sentence with correct preposition, 47
    complex sentences through context clues, 110
    negative statements using correct form of do, 38
    sentences using possessive adjectives, 36
    sentences using with correct form of present tense, 34
    sentences using with correct verb tense using adverbs and other context clues, 81
Create
    a personal time line, 59
    past tense questions for answers provided in text, 68

Define vocabulary, 60, 61, 76, 77, 106, 107,
Describe
    career activities using third-person singular present tense, 13
    people with adjectives based on context clues about their behaviors, 39

Disagree with a statement by using an opposite word, 88
Discuss
    potential careers and education necessary for those careers, 15
    what someone does using adverbs of frequency, 22
Distinguish between
    fact and opinion, 28, 83
    different sounds of simple past tense, 57
    present and present progressive tense, 18

Explain
    a pattern, 7
    a process, 87
Express likes and dislikes, 5

Give
    advice, 12, 21, 31, 43, 53, 64, 74, 84, 92, 102, 111,
    personal information, 1

Identify
    items that don't belong in a category, 23
    locations and careers from context clues, 109
Interpret
    a temperature chart and compute average temperatures, 104
    a weather map to answer questions about weather in different cities, 103

Label features on a map from written information, 96
Learn
    how to combine sentences, 78
    how to find the right volume of an encyclopedia, 62
    to alphabetize people's names, 52
    to alphabetize titles that start with A, An, or The, 82
    to classify books into the proper category, 100
    to use the index of a book to find information, 108
    to and give directions to specific locations, 98–99

Name
    careers from context clues, 16
    specific careers, 14
    specific items in a library, 79

Practice a dialogue, 79
Predict
    future actions based on specific situations, 48–49
    where an action is taking place based on context clues, 85
Provide
    antonyms for common vocabulary words, 86
    information about a school schedule, 75
Put statements in correct sequence, 8, 87

Rearrange statements to show a correct sequence, 51

Solve word problems using math terms, 66
Spell and pronounce past tense of verbs correctly, 56
State likes and dislikes, 7

Talk about
    career activities using present progressive tense, 17
    future plans using going to form, 44–45
    inaccuracies in a picture prompt, 10
    picture prompts using irregular past tense verb forms, 65
    picture prompts using simple past tense, 55
    two actions that happened in the past using simple past and past progressive, 69
Tell
    how people are feeling through the use of context clues, 72–73
    if a statement is true or false, 9
    what people are doing through the use of context clues, 41
    what people were doing through context clues, 101

Understand jokes and riddles, 54
Use
    a library card catalog to find books by title or author, 89
    context clues to complete sentences, 112, 113, 114
    guide words to locate dictionary items, 42
    rules to spell past tense verbs correctly, 58
Use correct form of have with singular and plural subjects, 29

Write
    a paragraph using third-person singular present tense verbs correctly, 35
    a short biography, 71, 97
    a short essay 80
        based on research, 83
        that provides context clues to tell how a person was feeling, 72, 73
        using geography terms, 94–95
        using information from a graph, 9
    about inaccuracies, 10
    about daily activities of a teacher, 16
    about two actions that happened in the past using simple past and past progressive, 70
    and pronounce third-person singular present tense verbs correctly, 33
    questions for specific statements, 4
    sentences using correct tense of the verb to be, 67